3.50

D0559102

Raymond Carver

Raymond

Carver

An Oral Biography

Sam Halpert

University of Iowa Press Ψ *Iowa City*

University
of Iowa Press,
Iowa City 52242
Copyright © 1995
by Sam Halpert
All rights reserved
Printed in the
United States
of America

Design by
Richard Hendel

No part of this book
may be reproduced or
used in any form or by
any means, electronic or
mechanical, including
photocopying and
recording, without
permission in writing
from the publisher.

Printed on acid-free paper

Library of Congress Cataloging-in-Publication Data

Halpert, Sam, 1920–

   Raymond Carver: an oral biography / by Sam
Halpert.

      p.   cm.

   Enl. ed. of: . . . When we talk about Raymond
Carver. 1st ed. 1991.

   ISBN 0-87745-502-3, ISBN 0-87745-503-1

   1. Carver, Raymond – Friends and associates –
Interviews.   2. Carver, Raymond – Criticism
and interpretation.   3. Authors, American –
20th century – Biography.   I. When we talk
about Raymond Carver.   II. Title.

PS3553.A7894Z69   1995

813'.54—dc20   94-46555

                                              CIP

01 00 99 98 97 96 95 C 5 4 3 2 1
01 00 99 98 97 96 95 P 5 4 3 2

Contents

Introduction

This book was originally intended as a reprint of . . . *When We Talk About Raymond Carver* (Gibbs Smith, 1991), a collection of conversations in interview form with Carver's writer friends and his first wife, Maryann. That earlier book, conceived as a tribute to Carver, was well received by readers and praised by critics; however, one year later the title was out of print.

In October 1993, the University of Iowa Press agreed to reprint the book with the addition of more interviews. After further discussion, we decided to publish a completely new edition rather than merely tacking on a set of new interviews. Though none of the original copy has been omitted, the earlier conversations have been rearranged and merged with the six new ones to flow with the perceived sequential patterns in Carver's life and work. All the new material comes from those who were close to Carver in the early Bad Raymond days. They bear witness to his struggles with the effects of alcoholism, the debt-ridden poverty, the constant moving from rented houses to apartments to trailer courts to motels, the bankruptcies, the grind of janitor jobs – the mother lode he mined and transformed into the art of those acclaimed stories.

The narratives often contradict each other in parts as the witnesses relate the same events from different points of view. Carver is the hero, the victim, and sometimes the villain in these tales spoken with affection as if at a wake. In writing about . . . *When We Talk About Raymond Carver*, Russell Banks first descried this imagery: "Appropriately and happily it's an old-fashioned Irish kind of wake, in which dear friends and family members gather and recollect and tell stories and lies, make their confessions and renew loyalties, offer toasts and sing songs of praise and lamentation, one hard upon another. Together, they conspire somehow to keep the beloved man around a little longer, fixing him vividly in language . . . before memory fades and all we have of him is the work itself, his marvelous stories and poems" (*Atlantic*, August 1991).

I regret the circumstances that prevented the inclusion of many who should have appeared in this book. Perhaps most conspicuously absent is Tess Gallagher. For the record, I did interview her for . . . *When We Talk About Raymond Carver.* She wrote many friendly notes expressing enthusiasm for the project before her final approval of the transcript, but shortly after the book was typeset and review copies had been sent out, her attorney informed me of her decision to withdraw her interview.

It should be noted that all the conversations were tape-recorded extemporaneously and unrehearsed. A transcript was prepared and sent to each interviewee. They were invariably returned with little delay and remarkably few revisions, many with enthusiastic messages of encouragement. All generously contributed time and effort in spirited appreciation and affection for Carver, the man, and his work.

This has been a most fulfilling venture for me and, no other way of saying it, a labor of love. Wherever I traveled, the message was out that Ray never felt happier, or more fortunate, than when sharing time with friends and fellow writers. So now let me raise my glass in special gratitude to those gathered here at the wake forthrightly offering up their tales of praise and lamentation. This book is my toast to the beloved man.

Raymond Carver

Dick Day

As soon as I saw his first manuscript I realized that this guy could really do something, because he had a strong sense of narrative. Of course a lot of writers have that, but not many know the other two things, and though one of them can be learned – the use of detail to establish a reality – the other I believe cannot be learned. It's the real gift, the true sign of whether a person is a writer or not – and that is the voice. And right from the start Ray's voice was authentic, personal, and compelling. A bit Hemingwayish maybe, but that's OK – you have to work through some predecessors.

The interview is held in Day's bare-bones cement-block office at Humboldt, a small state college up in the hills of Arcata, a coastal lumber mill town ringed by the vast towering redwood forests of northern California. Not many people up and about yet as the sun dries out the fog on a beautiful quiet Sunday morning. Richard Cortez Day is soft-spoken, reserved when he talks about Carver slowly, with affection, as if he were a favorite kid brother. He measures his words and pauses frequently as he recalls many hours spent with him in this small office when Ray was young and just starting out.

When did you and Ray Carver first cross paths?

Ray came to my creative writing class in 1961, transferring from Chico State, where he had spent a year studying under John Gardner. I'd known Gardner back at the University of Iowa Writers' Workshop. Ray came west here to Humboldt from Chico because he thought he'd land a job over here and help support his family.

He stayed here long enough to graduate, didn't he?

Oh yes, and over the time he was here he took five or six courses from me, including fiction writing. As soon as I saw his first manuscript I realized that this guy could really do something, because he had a strong sense of narrative. Of course a lot of writers have that, but not many know the other two things, and though one of them can be learned – the use of detail to establish a reality – the other I believe cannot be learned. It's the real gift, the true sign of whether a person is a writer or not – and that is the voice. And right from the start Ray's voice was authentic, personal, and compelling. A bit Hemingwayish maybe, but that's OK – you have to work through some predecessors.

What did he produce in your class?

A lot of what he wrote here came out in his stories later on. Although he wrote a story called "The Night the Mill Boss Died" which was obviously right out of his own experience, he was messing around a lot in Hemingway's tracks without having been where Hemingway went. He'd set a story in Mexico or Spain . . .

Not bullfight stories, please.

(Laughs) No, not that. He hadn't lived the experience, so I suggested he write stories a little closer to home. And he did. A lot of what he wrote about even then had to do with family, horrible jobs, people oppressed by their circumstances.

The theme of Carver stories later on?
Exactly.

Carver came into your class after a year at Chico with John Gardner. What effect would you say Gardner had on his work?

He learned the discipline of editing, of cutting, of getting it right. Of course Gardner didn't try to impose his vision or his manner of writing on Ray, but it was the craft of fiction that he learned from Gardner. If Ray had been a science fiction writer, Gardner would have done the same thing. Ray didn't have a philosophical bone in his body. He wasn't interested in larger structures of intangible ideas that governed the specific incidents or phenomena of his characters' life. That was not his business. That was for philosophers. John Gardner, Ph.D. in English, knew lots about abstruse subjects that Ray didn't care about. Ray was true to his own work and experience, and following that experience he drove home image after image. When you look at his stories as a whole, you see that they do intimate some attitudes toward the world. A philosophical position. Does that make sense to you?

Sure. Gardner was Gardner, and Carver was Carver. We can only write the way we are. Does that make sense?

That's true enough. The problem with realism is that I think people misunderstand what it is. Ray considered himself a realist writer, but reality depends on the angle of vision. What's real from here isn't real from over there. What's real in one mind or subjectivity is not real in another. So what a writer has to do is take his or her own sense of what's real and with the imagination make it absolutely convincing. As when Dylan Thomas writes a story called "The True Story" about a young woman who murders an old woman and then, having been caught, flies out the second-story window. The truth of "The True Story" and the seal upon its realism comes in the last line, where Thomas writes, "but Maria was not flying."

Well, we all see life through our own periscope, which gives a very narrow view, but it is our whole world. And locked in position by our experience, we can only write with that periscopal view.

Not only that, but we add our own emotional coloration to what we see. So what we describe depends in so many ways on how things are going in our lives.

Surely this applies to Ray.

This leads directly back to Ray. How does a writer find the details that make those emotions real? That's part of Ray's genius. Some little detail would pop up in his mind. A vacuum cleaner salesman, for example, would come into a character's house and find all kinds of detritus and other filth. Now did such a salesman ever come to Ray's house? Maybe yes, maybe no, but in the story Ray takes him all the way, gives the salesman full scope, and by those imagined details gives the emotional definition of a man whose wife has left him. His life is in shambles.

Did you see much of Ray outside of class?

Oh sure. We found all kinds of reasons to celebrate in those days. Ray would get a story or poem published, or I would, and then we would all get together and there would be food on the table and we would drink. Those times were absolutely delightful. Anything was possible it seemed. It wasn't unusual for Ray to call me in the middle of the night, or I to call him, to meet to talk about a story one of us had just finished. We'd go to an all-night cafe and drink coffee and tell tall tales and have a good time. Alcohol was around, but it was not a huge problem. It was mostly for celebrating. Other things that were not so good were happening too. Ray and Maryann had very little money. They were struggling to get on.

Ray was a full-time student with a wife and two children. What did he do for money?

Ray was holding one crap job or another briefly, but the mainstay and the dynamo that ran the family was Maryann. She was a genius at finding work. I used to say that if you parachuted her blindfolded into a city where she'd never been, within twenty minutes she'd find a job doing something that would bring in money for the family. She was good at that here. For example, she'd get a job at a pancake house and she'd make more tips on a shift than you would think possible. And you increase the possibilities when you see her working as a cocktail waitress dealing with businessmen in bars charming them into generosity. She could find a job as a waitress in two seconds flat.

At the same time, she was a student here at Humboldt. She'd enroll for some classes and was at least in one of my classes with Ray. And Maryann always wrote A papers. She had a keen analytical mind and was a first-rate student. Ray, on the other hand, though he was enormously intelligent and could write superb papers, had another agenda. If writing a paper conflicted with the time he wanted to work on a story, he'd ignore the paper and do the story. Ray didn't know how to deal with the world. He was shy, inward. There were times, when given the general pressures of life, Ray would go into a room, lock the door, and keep the kids and everybody else out while he'd lie there in the dark with the covers pulled up over his eyes for a long time. The world was just too much for him. He didn't know how to deal with it, but Maryann did. She was the one who dealt with the world for the family.

Paid the bills?

Paid the bills, you bet. Put food on the table and did everything she could to further Ray's reputation.

How would you describe Ray at that point in his life?

He was almost perilously thin, tall, stooped. He had blue eyes, deep blue. He wore horn-rimmed eyeglasses, the lenses of which stopped most people's vision. You didn't really see the eyes unless you looked for them through the glass, and then you'd notice that they were intensely watchful. They weren't missing a thing.

How was he in class?

He was never one to go to the center of any kind of activity. I always thought of him as one who would skirt around the edges but would overhear all kinds of things, never miss a nuance. He wasn't a very strong person. There was a physical education requirement here at Humboldt at the time. He signed up for the required class, which turned out to be in weight lifting, and he just couldn't lift anything. So he dropped that class and exchanged it for a class in bowling. He got through that one, but barely.

How did he interact with the other students?

He made friends with other students, but it was always a quiet friendship. People liked him a lot, even though he was quite shy. He had inexplicable fears as well, amounting to paranoia. In the house they were living in, which was on a street leading to the high school, Ray always kept the window shades pulled down to the bottom. If you'd knock on the door, you'd see the shade part a crack, enough to see the eyeball behind it.

Was that fear of bill collectors?

Fear of the outside world. A fear that there were conspiracies afoot against him. He was even afraid of the high school students passing the house on their way to school. Afraid they were going to lay siege to the house, and he'd peep from behind the shade, watching these harmless students going by. He also thought the draft was after him at one point.

But he had a wife and two children at the time.

Yes, and he had bad eyes and he wasn't in any physical shape at all, but at one point he had some kind of intimation that he might be drafted. He showed up at my house with a little one-by-two suitcase packed. Take me someplace, he said, to wherever. He had enough in that suitcase to last about an hour and a half. I had a tough time finally talking him out of it, and of course nothing ever came of it. You have to understand that Ray was not above any chicanery or deception to escape something as onerous as the draft or, for that matter, anything else he wished to evade.

You are not the first to tell me that. Although people loved him, there is a perception that he often seemed to operate under his own set of rules.

Well, he did. When he was younger and going through his bad period, you could see his definition in that way. It was interesting to watch what happened later when he got off the booze and put on some physical substance, a little weight on those bones. He always was tall and over the years he became a big man in more ways than one. He became much more generous to people, much more affable, much less nervous and paranoid on the surface.

That's what poverty will do to you. It's hard to be generous when you have nothing to share. Didn't Ray say something to the effect that there was nothing much wrong with him in those days that a little money couldn't cure?

Yes, he did. It takes a lot of reconditioning to escape those feelings of poverty. You learn that it's a dog-eat-dog world on the bottom level, and you never forget it.

You encouraged Ray to go on to the Iowa Workshop. Was he eager to go there?

He was quite eager, as I remember it. His first mentor, which is the right word, had come straight from the Iowa Workshop to Chico State. Ray admired John Gardner and learned much from him there. Though I can't say how much Ray learned from me, I too wasn't long out of Iowa. I still knew some people there. I wrote, I think, to Don Justice, saying in effect that Ray Carver was the real thing. I urged that he be admitted to the workshop, and I urged that he be given financial support. Of course, it wasn't my letter that tipped the scales. It was the quality of the stories Ray submitted. I should also say that, already heading for the big world as a writer, Ray saw the Iowa Workshop as the right place to go next, and I saw things the same way.

Donald Justice

I had read some of his stories and poems and I thought he was very talented, but I didn't realize, and I'm not sure anyone did, how good he was going to be. Have you come across anyone who in '72 knew how successful he would become?

The interview takes place in the living room of Justice's comfortable house overlooking the Iowa River. Through the picture window, we see an eagle sailing broad-winged slowly over the snow-covered river. It is a gray January day in Iowa City. Justice smiles often while recalling Carver's days in and out of the Iowa Workshop. We admire the grace of the eagle as it glides, darkly profiled against the bare branches of the trees lining the bank on the far side of the river.

Was it here at Iowa where you first met Ray Carver?

Yes, it was in the early sixties. He was a student in the poetry workshop I was teaching, and about all I recall from that time is that he was dissatisfied and restless. He felt the workshop atmosphere was wrong for him, and it probably was. He left after no more than a semester, as I recall. This was about '63 or '64. Years later he told me that his memory of the place wasn't all that bad.

Well, he came back many times. When did you next see him?

In the early seventies, when he came back to teach fiction here.

What do you recall about him from this period?

I'd see him around the offices quite a bit. Our paths crossed mostly in socializing, at parties. I remember a poker game in his room in the Iowa House one Sunday evening in which I lost heavily. Ray bluffed me out of a couple of hands.

Did you work with him in any way?

I remember consulting with him on some of the application manuscripts. We were always swamped with manuscripts from people applying to come here as students. Marvin Bell and I asked him if he would help out a little on the poetry applications, which he very kindly did.

Anything more?

Not much. He just seemed to be like one of the guys. We were all teaching together in the same program and we liked Ray and thought it was great that he was here, but nothing of any particular significance happened that I saw or knew about. I think Cheever was here at the same time and I'm sure they became friendly.

Did you see much of them together?

As it happened I didn't meet Cheever at that time. I met him later, but he was around. He was the famous story writer and Ray was scarcely known. I suppose he was as well known here in Iowa City as he was anywhere. It would be some years more in fact before Ray would be generally recognized as a writer.

Had you read any of his work at the time? What did you think of it?

I had read some of his stories and poems and I thought he was very talented, but I didn't realize, and I'm not sure anyone did, how good he was going to be. Have you come across anyone who in '72 knew how successful he would become?

John Leggett

I was a little apprehensive when I first set eyes on him. He seemed to be this big sort of lumbering cow-pokey kind of guy. A total contrast

to Cheever, urbane in his Brooks Brothers clothes, while Ray was tousled and frazzled, kind of bleary-eyed. I think he always wore these western shirts, plaid shirts with a drawstring around the collar, but you couldn't help liking him. He was so friendly. At first I thought, This has to be some sort of cover, but it wasn't. It was the real Ray. He was kind and generous and gentle. A huge gentleman.

The interview takes place after breakfast in Leggett's home high in the hills above Napa. Each window affords a splendid panoramic view of the valley spread below. Leggett informs me that on a clear day you can see San Francisco forty miles to the south. He is a generous, cheerful, lively spirited man and obviously enjoys narrating his recollections of the Bad Raymond days at the Iowa Workshop.

When and how did you first meet Ray Carver?

Raymond Carver first entered my life in 1971, I believe. I had been the director of the Iowa Writers' Workshop a couple of years, and one of the things that we had just begun was the Iowa short fiction contest. It was started by John Simmons, who was then director of the University of Iowa Press, and Vance Bourjaily, who was the reason I went to Iowa originally. The idea was that we would welcome short story manuscripts and publish the best collection with a prize of five hundred dollars or possibly even a thousand, and we'd do the semifinal evening at the workshop. I and the other members of the staff would read them.

How did you choose the winner?

We received a lot of manuscripts – several hundred. So that there'd be no favoritism, we would select and pay distinguished off-campus authors to make the final decision of ten manuscripts. I think the major readers were Joyce Carol Oates in '72 and Jack Hawkes in '73. I used to dread this stuff because all I was doing was reading these manuscripts in addition to my student manuscripts. It was just one more pile of manuscripts I had to haul, but I remember coming across a collection by a man named Raymond Carver of whom I'd never heard before and I was arrested. I was so astonished by this manuscript that I called my friend Simmons and said, We've got it, John, this is terrific. So off it went to the judge.

Was this the collection that was later published as Will You Please Be Quiet, Please?

I think so, but it may have been altered. I didn't read every story, but I remember reading three of these stories. They were so much better than any of the other stuff I'd been reading that I knew I didn't have to read another one. It was like panning for gold, and there you have a nugget. So I was stunned when I found the judge had awarded the prize to a writer whom I dare say you may have never heard of.

Who was the judge?

I believe the judge that year was Joyce Carol Oates. Yes, I know that because I just checked that out yesterday.

Isn't that something? I know for a fact that she is a great admirer of Carver's work.

And of course so is Jack Hawkes, whom I'll speak of later in this interview. Incidentally, years later after Ray was a successful Mercedes-driving author with money coming out of his ears, I remember asking him who were those two judges that turned you down. I'll bet they're really smarting. Of course he knew perfectly well, but he said, I don't have any grudges and I don't want you to have any either. I thought, There's a really Christian man *(chuckles)* glowing with human kindness now that he's so rich.

In any case, I was stunned by the decision, but I thought, Maybe I'm wrong. I'm wrong most of the time anyway. So a year went by, I was sitting in the same chair out in my house on Summit Street in Iowa City reading another pile of manuscripts. And there it was again! The Carver stories. I thought, God, a second chance. Isn't this marvelous? We lost this wonderful long fish and here he is swimming right back in our net.

I immediately called Simmons and said, This time I know the guy is going to win. That year the off-campus judge was Jack Hawkes and he awarded the prize to another writer whose name may not ring loudly in your ears. I was so furious at this choice that I felt I had to do something about it this time. I was so thwarted.

Had you written or contacted Carver by then?

Up to then, no, not at all. I didn't know anything about Carver but his name and address. I called him, and I think he was at Santa Cruz then. I got him on the line and said, It's a terrible thing. This is twice you've struck out, and I think we're really wrong here, but there isn't too much I can do about it. I can't reverse the judge's decision, we pay him to make these judgments, but would you want to come here and teach. He said, Yeah, right, when do we go and how much do you pay. It was agreed and it was the same year John Cheever was teaching here. We knew who Cheever was and we felt lucky to get him, but Carver was a complete unknown to us. It was just on a hunch that this guy was so good that we had to do something for him, that I had to act on my grievance about the way things had gone.

What was your reaction when he showed up?

I was a little apprehensive when I first set eyes on him. He seemed to be this big sort of lumbering cow-pokey kind of guy. A total contrast to Cheever, urbane in his Brooks Brothers clothes, while Ray was tousled and frazzled, kind of bleary-eyed. I think he always wore these western shirts, plaid shirts with a drawstring around the collar, but you couldn't help liking him. He was so friendly. At first I thought, This has to be some sort of cover, but it wasn't. It was the real Ray. He was kind and generous and gentle. A huge gentleman.

But he was drunk, wasn't he?

Drunk? Yes, but everybody drank. Cheever had just had a massive heart attack, but he was out drinking more than any of us and misbehaving with the students all the time. The fall semester was under way two or three weeks when somebody in Ray's section said that Ray isn't here. I said, What do you mean he isn't here. He said, Ray has gone back to Santa Cruz. I said, Do you mean for the weekend. No, he said, he's gone back to teaching there. I said, How could he be there teaching when he's supposed to be here teaching for us? We have a contract with him. His students were very loyal to him, but it came out that he taught two or three weeks for us, but he hadn't quit his job at Santa Cruz. I'm told that he also wangled a pass with the airlines and had arranged a captain's paradise. I have no idea how this was all resolved, but I do know that we were happy that he hung around enough not only for the fall semester but on into the following spring semester. Everybody had a great time, and bit by bit he developed a tremendous following among the students. He and Cheever got along beautifully. We all enjoyed him.

Could you tell us more about the Carver/Cheever connection?

Ray and Cheever astonished me by getting along like pals. I remember them coming to my house for dinner, walking up the path like Mutt and Jeff, laughing together. I had thought that Cheever would be hostile to this guy, but he always spoke very favorably of Ray to me. Certainly Ray must have been in awe of Cheever. It was a very good year, and certainly for the workshop, to have those two guys around. It was in many ways a banner year. Of course Cheever was making waves and causing all kinds of gossip. He'd been entertained by everybody on campus, parties were given for him, and he was always out to dinner, and he decided to throw a big party at the faculty club at Iowa House. His wife, Mary, came out from New York for the celebration, and we all wondered what he was going to do with her because John had been having an affair with a student in his class. Well, the party was well under way before he made his appearance with his girlfriend on one arm and his wife, Mary, on the other. Mary was wearing the longest, darkest mink coat I'd ever seen. People in Iowa City had never seen a mink coat, and here was John with a lumberjack's girlfriend on one arm and his wife in mink on the other.

Did you see Ray after that spring semester?

Yes, about a year later, a smaller version of Ray, John Jackson, one of his favorite drinking companions and former student of Ray's, dropped by the office and said, You've got to bring Ray back here for a reading. So I was persuaded to book Ray back here for a reading.

When was the reading to take place?

This would be late in the spring of '74. This turned out to be a kind of festival. Everybody was glad he was coming, and his former students and drinking buddies were all out to meet him. Ray arrived, to my surprise, three or four days ahead of the scheduled date for the reading, which concerned me. I wondered what kind of trouble he'd get into before the actual reading. I'd get periodical reports, and Ray would come in looking a little more delicate each morning but still ambulatory, though getting worse. By the morning of the reading I received an anxious call from John Jackson saying, I don't think Ray's going to be able to read tonight. He's really out and has the worst hangover in the world and is about to start drinking again. There's no possibility of us pulling him up on the stage tonight, so how about postponing it for a week. Nothing doing, I said. I knew if Ray stayed in the hands of John Jackson for another week, there'd be no more Ray Carver readings ever. I told Jackson that Ray was going to read that night even if the two of us had to hold him up. Later I received reports that black coffee was going down and Ray was propped up in the shower and had announced he was OK and he'd be able to read. So the great event occurred in a big hall crammed with students, people in the doorways, and Ray whispering hoarsely to me, Jack, I'm sure I'm going to be all right. I introduced him and he began to read and it came out in a whisper so low and hoarse that despite our turning the volume on the microphone all the way up, not a word could be heard.

His mind seemed to be working fine, and presumably he was reading the words, but he had lost his voice. Of course, we didn't know that, and Ray assumed the microphone was amplifying his whisper because everybody out there was eagerly leaning forward to hear him. He read a full forty-five minutes or so, then smiled and bowed to thunderous applause. Nobody had heard a word. He came off the stage beaming and said,

How was I, Jack? I shook his hand and said, Ray, you were grand.

It's amazing that he received such a reception. Only a few of his stories had been published at the time.

These were his friends – the students, the faculty. He was already a legendary drinker and friend and counselor. He was regarded as a man with a great talent for analyzing other people's stories and spending the time to talk to them about it.

I'm sure that wasn't his last stand here.

Oh yes. After he had become successful he came back to Iowa several times. I always had great affection for him and was so pleased to see that he had gone off the booze and had developed a lasting relationship with Tess Gallagher, who had been a poet at the workshop, though he didn't meet her here. She seemed to me to be a good woman, and they were devoted to one another so far as I know. I remember him telling me about his success with modesty and a slight chuckle. It was wonderful to talk about this with someone who had been in such need and living on the ragged edge of survival. He'd tripped the latch of foundation grants and money was no longer a problem. He no longer needed Iowa as a solace or a place to pick up a little reading money.

William Kittredge

I remember Ray and me sitting at a bar in Missoula when a woman bartender told us about being arrested the night before because she and her boyfriend got stoned and moved all their furniture out on the lawn, set up lights and all. After awhile the neighbors got annoyed and called the cops. I looked at Ray and told him that had to be his. So he wrote it, changed it a little. The one about the guy moving all his stuff out in the driveway for a yard sale?

The interview takes place at the Yarrow Hotel in Park City, Utah, where Kittredge is to give a reading at the Writers at Work conference. I usually find it advisable to chat for a few moments as a warm-up before starting the tape, but I can skip the blather with Bill. He's as comfortable and easy as an old shoe.

We adjourn to the bar after the interview, and he runs off a few stories. I recall talking with him in Aspen on the day we heard that Ray had died. I'll not soon forget the unsentimental, simple manner in which Bill expressed his feelings of loss that day for his dear friend.

We all know that you and Ray were good friends, but in the beginning . . .

Well, it's real clear. I can be specific because I remember it so vividly. It was during spring break 1970, I was teaching at the University of Montana, and the woman who was my wife at that time and I went to Seattle, you know, just to get out of Montana and hang around for awhile at the Olympic, one of the old grand hotels. They were having one of those college English teachers' conventions there, whatever the acronym is. The place was pretty near empty. I don't remember what the meeting was about, but it was something like nine o'clock at night, and they had these long book stalls with all the publishers' books lined up. Maybe two hundred yards of book stalls and nobody around at all. The place is empty and I'm walking around and looking at these books and trying to resist the impulse to heist a couple of them. My wife and I and a guy way down at the far end were the only ones around. Anyway, I picked up a copy of a book edited by Curt Johnson, who incidentally was the publisher of the journal where "Will You Please Be Quiet, Please?" first appeared. I was browsing through the book when this guy walks up. He's kind of a scruffy-looking guy, looks over my shoulder and says, "I've got a story in there." My first impulse was to say something like "Yeah, I'll bet you have." In any event, we kind of jousted about for a minute or two, and then it turned out it was Ray. I couldn't believe anyone would claim that story if it weren't really theirs. So then we started talking, and he told me he had read a couple stories that I had written, which made him one of the few people in the world I had met that had ever laid eyes on a story of mine. Then we had some coffee and talked some more and someone said, Let's have a beer, so we went to the bar and someone said, Let's have a drink. Next thing I know we're just plastered.

I'm glad you're able to remember it so well.

We kind of met as aspiring writers. I was a lot more aspiring than he was, because he had achieved some success by then. But also we met as drunks, essentially. We were supposed to get together and have dinner the next night, but that didn't work out. I didn't see him again until I got back to Montana. Maybe about a month later I get a letter from this guy and he says he wants to come up and visit. I'm not exactly sure when it was, sometime around in the fall of '70. He and Maryann came from Palo Alto on the train. He came to Montana and I couldn't figure why this guy wanted to do that. I think at this time he felt very isolated.

Why? What was going on in his life at the time?

That was around the year that he stayed home from work for the whole winter and Maryann taught school in Los Altos while he wrote all those stories that were first published in *Esquire* like "Neighbors" and all those. In those seven or eight months he wrote about twelve stories, all of which were published and all well known today, but he felt really isolated, and I think he was just looking for someone to hang out with. Someone to drink with.

How did the visit go?

He came to Missoula, stuck around four or five days, stayed at our house, and met a bunch of the writers there. We had a big time and then he went back. After – I'm not sure of my chronology here, things sort of overlap. By then we were big chums. My ex-wife and I went down to visit him at his house, he was living then in Mountain View. We met Maryann's sister Amy, who is now married to Doug Unger. Again it was all more big parties. We were roaring along and having high times. There were lots of what we thought of at that time as great adventures. There was this whole system of camaraderie set up.

And how about other visits?

He came back to Missoula and we went back down to visit

him. Then in '72–'73 he received a Stegner fellowship at Stanford. The next year I had one, probably due in part because Ray put in a good word for me. I went down around June of '73 and again more big times. By then the marriage I had was really on the rocks and –

Ray's wasn't doing too well either, I guess.
Well, it came and went in all kinds of ways, but it endured longer than anybody ever thought it would considering the circumstances.

What happened then?
I went down and stayed with him for a few days, then rented a place and lived there. That was the time Ray was flying back and forth between teaching in Iowa City and Santa Cruz. I and some of his friends would go down and get him off the plane on Thursday afternoon. He'd always come home loaded, and on Friday he'd be supposed to teach at Santa Cruz. A couple of times he made it, but most of the time we'd pin a note on the door saying Mr. Carver is too sick to teach, and it was true. Then he began to not show up at all. Chuck Kinder and I went down once to teach the class together and it was a disaster. I think Ray must have met that class about twice. The provost of the college got wind of what was going on and of Ray also teaching at Iowa City. They fired him, and deservedly so. I don't know what happened to the class and the students. It was a long, dark, hard period for Ray.

Leonard Michaels

Michaels: Well, what can I say? When he was low, he got drunk.
When I was low, I read Hegel.
Halpert: Hegel! *(Laughs)* You had no other choice?
Michaels: Well, neither of us were too happy at the time.

The interview begins in Michaels's office at the University of California in Berkeley. It is a small, utilitarian room; unpretentious, books on shelves floor to ceiling, overflowing onto three chairs and a desk with a portable typewriter in the center of the room. After a short break for lunch, we continue the interview at his small, comfortable house in Kensington, a few minutes' drive from campus. We are greeted by his eleven-year-old daughter, who gives her dad an affectionate hug and kiss. Michaels beams as he embraces his favorite critic.

When and where did you first meet Ray?

I don't remember exactly when, but he was in my living room, here in Kensington, sometime in the early seventies. He got in touch with me. He got in touch because we had friends in common and he said he'd like to visit. I think that's how it went. I said sure and he came by. Here was this very nicely dressed, very composed – and, it seemed to me, tensely restrained – soft-spoken man, a little on the burly side perhaps. I remember him sitting in the living room, staring at me, waiting for something to be said, or something to happen. He had this quality of patient waiting, not putting himself forward, letting you determine the direction of talk. He wore a gray tweed jacket, I believe. He also wore a tie and neatly pressed pants. I might have taken him for a businessman, maybe an insurance salesman. His composure, his conventional clothes – as if he'd come for a job interview. I can't remember one word of our conversation, but he made a very good impression. A solid kind of guy. Salt of the earth. I never met anyone who seemed more *normal*.

Had you read any of his stories prior to meeting him?

I can't recall, but I must have read a story or two and thought they were good. Around then I was editing a magazine called *Occident*, or acting as one of the editors. It was the U of Cal literary, the oldest literary journal in the state. I asked Ray to give us a story.

Did you publish it?

Yes. It was his early work, and I liked it a lot. I liked his sense of humor and the way he managed to suppress a certain element of rationality, so the events in a story would move forward by virtue of a subconscious compulsion. As if there were no reality principle. This is too complicated and I don't like to talk this way. There was a craziness in his stories that pleased me. I never made the connection between his stories – how they move from the normal to the weirdly extravagant – and his personality. On some level I felt the dynamic in them and him, and I liked it.

And after that . . .

After that Ray needed a job. I used what influence I had to get him something here at Berkeley. Then I tried to make Berkeley extend itself and keep him on, give him some kind of security, but that didn't work out. He wasn't a star, he wasn't fashionable, he didn't have a Ph.D., he was just another writer coming up. Besides, there was opposition from one of my fellow writers in the department. He said his work was remorselessly downbeat. It should have been more cheery and optimistic, maybe like Beckett and Kafka. The more people attacked Ray, the more I realized he was an important writer.

And after that . . .

After that I tried to help Ray get a Guggenheim fellowship. I typed out a long letter, essentially saying that I was aware the foundation didn't usually grant fellowships the first time somebody applied for one, but let me try to tell you what I believe is important about his writing. My point was that this is rare and this should be supported. I thought I'd written the most irresistible plea ever. *(Laughter. Pause)* If you look at Ray's first book you'll see an endorsement from just one writer.

Well, we know you're the world's greatest critic.

(Laughter) *Did Ray do well after the book came out?*

Yes, but there were heavy blows at first. A number of established sensibilities didn't want him in the city. There's a Russian saying: When you enter the city, the geese begin to cackle. But then some big names weighed in on his side. Soon thereafter right opinion seized the mental masses, high and low.

What did you think of his work after that?

There are impressive stories early and late, but I like the early stuff – a lot of it anyway – best. It had a wild, musical quality. Like poetry, but you know you don't find much of this wildness in Ray's poetry.

Do you find that note missing in his later work?

No, it's not missing. It's just that his work becomes deeper, almost as if he begins to feel what he feels, so the meaning of the stories is *in* the stories, whereas in the first book the meaning can wait. Do you see what I mean? The story has trajectory. The meaning can come along later. It's not so involved in the experience of the story itself. Take a late story like "Intimacy," where Ray is being naughty, isn't he? I mean the naughty character who resembles Ray in the story, and Ray himself, outside the story. The feeling of all that is part of the story's self-consciousness. Maybe if I didn't know the people I wouldn't find it problematic, or maybe the story is disturbing to me just because it is a good story. His later work is, for all I know, superior. I'm talking about what I like. I'm not talking about what's good or bad in the eye of God.

Are you saying his early work is more visceral? Purer?

It's more musical. To my ear. More terrifying. Terrifying in the Kierkegaardian sense, like life itself. I don't know *(laughs)*, forget that.

You also knew him on a personal level?

We were friends. I didn't see him regularly over a long period, but he invited me to parties at his house, and I invited him to parties in Berkeley, and there were other occasions when we talked, just talked without any formal context.

What was your sense of him, let's say, when you met him at a party?

My sense of him was that he was often drunk – not in a flamboyant way, just a little sodden. I never saw him become angry or violent. He always remained pleasant, even funny, except one time in Santa Cruz. I remember him slumped in a big chair in the living room of his house while the party was going full blast, and he was gloomily studying the crowd, the people dancing. He dealt with alcoholism in his stories. I assume it's his own experience. I don't mean he's writing exactly what it is that happens to him in the course of his own life. He may well have done that, for all I know, but he obviously was using his knowledge of certain kinds of experience at a very deep level. The stories do have that sort of confessional force. This is – what can I say – *(pause)* an argument for some people and I don't think it should *(pause)* . . .

An argument for what?

You know, people whisper that the story is the truth, or it's based on reality and so on and so forth, and you're supposed to believe that the story is less of an achievement somehow, that it's less of a creative thing. Well, the quality of a story is in *how* it is written, not what the story is about; anyway stories just don't come out of nowhere, like the world came out of nowhere. Before God came along, there was nothing. God didn't have any experience, right?

Maybe that's what's wrong with the world . . .

(Laughs) Wait until the next time around. It's going to be terrific!

In the revision?

Yes, it's all in the rewrite.

What else was going on in his life at the time?

Well, I heard that he was teaching at Iowa and Santa Cruz without informing either school about his job at the other. He even managed to con United into flying him for free, telling them he'd put United into his stories. Of course he never wrote a word about them. He also had a lover in Denver where he changed planes. So there he was, holding on to two teaching jobs a couple of thousand miles apart, and drinking, and carrying on a love affair, and conning United into flying him back and forth. Anyway that's what I heard. There's much more gossip, but it has no real relation to his writing. It's just life. Material. Stuff. Of interest to media-besotted types who can't read.

How were you getting along with him at that time?

Well, there was a party – it was right after the publication of my second book. Ray drew me aside and told me straight out exactly what he didn't like in the book. He didn't like the literary allusions, references to philosophers, or explicit statement of ideas. I'd heard this before from other writers. These things in my writing took away from the brainless pitch of reality. There was no drama or pleasure in them. Why did I do it? Ray disapproved. I had done it for a reason other than he imagined. It was intended to represent states of depression, not intellectuality. He hurt my feelings, especially since he'd once said I was an influence on his own writing, but my point in telling this is to show how he was changing, gaining confidence. Anyway this is not about me.

But it is, you and Ray.
Well, what can I say? When he was low, he got drunk. When I was low, I read Hegel.

Hegel! (Laughs) *You had no other choice?*
Well, neither of us were too happy at the time.

Did he have more than a drinking problem at that time?
I spent afternoons and evenings with him and Maryann, and I could see the kind of trouble they were having, but I also saw that they were deeply connected in ways that are almost impossible to describe. They were very close. I can't get into this. I can't say what goes on in anybody's marriage in the real world. I make things up when I write, but there were things that I could see about that marriage that suggested to me however bad it may have been, the very badness came out of some tremendously deep, intimate, absolute condition. Something very important to both of them, but they were both involved in it. I loved them both and I saw they had trouble, and I saw they were deeply – and it looked to me permanently – connected.

Was Maryann with him at these parties during the Bad Raymond days?
Yes. He was always with Maryann. There was one time he arrived with Maryann, Bill Kittredge, Doug Unger, and I don't know who else. This was at the party celebrating Ray's story in *Occident*. I remember they came walking in, Maryann first, and she was clearly bombed out of her mind. I thought she had arrived alone, but ten seconds later Kittredge came

walking in, also bombed, and both of them smiling in a pleasing drunken way, and I thought, well, at least Kittredge and Maryann arrived. Next thing I know, along comes Unger. Now all these people had come together to the party, but they were walking in at ten-second intervals, and not as a joke. This was just how they were arriving in their separate little worlds, and finally along comes Ray smiling just the way he always smiled. There they were *(laughs)* one after the other in single file shuffling across the room to say hello. I almost always saw him with Maryann.

With all that drunkenness, how do you suppose he was able to create all those fine stories?

He found the material for his stories in the things that were happening to him, the things he was seeing, and feeling. The people he dealt with and lived with were all participants in a way in his writing. I imagine Maryann lived through a hell of a lot of that material with him, and I suspect that she *and* Ray paid for those stories with their lives.

Could you tell us a bit more about Maryann?

She was always quick to say what she thought when she didn't like something. A writer's name would come up and she might say, "There's nobody home," meaning the work was shit. Ray never disagreed, but he wouldn't put himself on record – at least not around me. He was cautious, diplomatic. Saying what you think, even in the most innocent circumstances, can come back to haunt you later. Maryann wasn't diplomatic. She was strong, forthright, even a little fierce. As far as I could tell, she was right in her judgments. Ray was lucky to have her reading his work, just to keep it free of schmaltz and manipulation.

Douglas Unger

Maryann had heard of a place called Duffy's, an alcoholic rehabilitation center in Myrtledale, California. She was selling the house in Cupertino and had scraped together the money for a rehab center for Ray. This place, Duffy's, is the model for Frank Martin's in "Where I'm

Unger welcomes me on the front porch of the small house that he and his wife, Amy, occupy just off the Syracuse campus. She asks me whether I intend to interview her sister Maryann Carver. I'd been strongly considering that possibility since the Michaels and Kittredge interviews, but neither of them had any idea where she might be or if she'd be willing to participate in an interview. She'd never spoken to anyone for publication. Amy offers to help me take care of that little problem.

It's a quiet Saturday summer afternoon in Syracuse. Quiet but for the clatter of a neighbor mowing his lawn. Doug and I go inside for the interview. He offers me a cold beer. Two guys in shirtsleeves, sitting at a dining room table and talking into a small tape recorder. They smile from time to time. The bright afternoon sun recedes behind the neighbor's house, casting long shadows across the table. The mowing stops. The guys keep on. They are having a serious talk.

Do you remember how you first met Ray?

I like to think back to the first occasion that I met Ray through his writing, much before I actually met Ray Carver the man. It was when I was the managing editor of the *Chicago Review* and the story "They're Not Your Husband" came into the office –

What year was this?

The fall of '73. And the way I discovered Ray's work was the unusual way that manuscript came to the office. In those days we were generally getting piles of submissions every month through the mail, really more than we could read seriously. But this story came in hand carried by the editor, Richard Hack. He had just been given the story by Curt Johnson of December Press, who I believe had the story passed on to him at a writers' conference in Wisconsin. So I had the impression that Ray Carver stories were being passed on like that, in a kind of wonderful underground way, all around the country. We read that story with excitement, right away, that minute, because it came to us like that, and we discovered that "They're Not Your Husband" seemed to be something entirely new in those days.

New? In what way new?

Back then in the early seventies, the editorial focus and the majority of the manuscripts we were reading seemed to be of a kind of so-called experimental fiction that Ray later often spoke out against – highly textured prose, with highly innovative and surreal subjects, a fiction called metafiction, as in the styles of Pynchon and Coover, and Barth and Barthelme and Hawkes; writers who were very much in vogue then. "They're Not Your Husband" was nothing like that. It was a straightforward story, realistic, with an unadorned style that also had a lot of humor in its implications. There was also a very strange dark quality to the writing that I felt myself immediately drawn to. As I remember it, Richard Hack and I and some of the staff decided to accept the story that same day. We had never acted that quickly before. That was my introduction to Ray's writing. I had no way of knowing that later I'd not only meet the man but also become part of his family.

How did you follow up your early interest in his work?

I heard a lot about Ray and read as many of his stories as I could find when I was at the Iowa Workshop. There were all kinds of tales about him. Let's just say that he had cut a swath in Iowa City. But the students all loved him and couldn't praise him enough. He and John Cheever had been famously drunk together in Iowa City on many an occasion, and the workshop was still recovering.

Cheever and Carver – their names go together, right out of Dickens. Did they in fact get along?

Ray admired John Cheever's writing. And I know they became fast friends almost immediately, and it was a great literary friendship.

What was Ray's status as a writer at that time?

By the time Ray arrived at Iowa, he'd been writing serious fiction for at least fourteen years. He'd been published in many fine literary journals. He had received prizes and was anthologized – *The Best Short Stories of '67*, *The Best Little Magazine Fiction of '71 and '72*, and in the O. Henry award stories. He had at that point two stories published or accepted by Gordon Lish at *Esquire*. But he'd reached a kind of ending point both in his life and his writing. He was perhaps at one of the lowest points in his life, and he was still sinking.

What was the main problem?

A good part of the problem was money. He was terribly broke and had declared bankruptcy. In those days Ray often used to say, "I never had a problem that money couldn't solve." But I think a bigger problem was that no publisher anywhere in the country would accept his book, *Will You Please Be Quiet, Please?* The collection represented fourteen years of work. Still, editors found the stories too depressing, or not in tune with what the culture wanted to read, and the book wouldn't sell. Short story collections were very hard to get published back then. For one reason or another he was turned down, time and again. The way he came to teach in Iowa –

Was that his first time at Iowa?

No, he had been a student there years before. Most people aren't aware that Ray had been a student in poetry at the Iowa Writers' Workshop when Paul Engle was the director in '63 and '64. And Engle didn't renew Ray's financial aid. Ray was so shy back then. He'd had poems published, and at least one long story called "Furious Seasons," which he had used as part of his application to Iowa. But he wasn't the kind to show off his work easily. He was very quiet in the workshops. Engle hadn't noticed him or his work and didn't renew Ray's financial aid for the second year.

Ray was married and had two young children and responsibilities. You get a picture of all this in his essay "Fires," in the description of running the laundry through, at the mercy of the "law of the laundromat" he calls it, and of his terrible frustration, wishing for writing time and feeling that his life is a small-change thing. One thing that's not said in "Fires" is how good a father Ray was then. He took care of the kids a lot. His wife, Maryann, worked as a full-time waitress at the Athletic Club to pay the bills. Not getting aid was a crushing blow.

After all that, how did he come to teach at Iowa?

That's a kind of sad story. He had sent *Will You Please Be Quiet, Please?* in to the Iowa Short Fiction Award contest. Even though the preliminary judges selected his book to win, for some reason their decision was reversed and it didn't win. Jack Leggett, who was director of the workshop, was outraged at that decision. He was so outraged that he told everyone that not only did he think that Ray's manuscript should have won first prize hands down but that he was going to offer Ray a teaching job. So he invited Ray to teach the following year.

Then how did you finally get to meet Ray?

I met Ray through my wife, Amy, three months after I met her. Ray's wife then, Maryann, is Amy's sister. I fell in love with Amy at Iowa in the fall of '75, when I was a teaching fellow at the workshop, and she was finishing her M.F.A. in acting. Ray's name began to come up, and I began hearing a lot of the family stories about him. Especially how concerned Amy was for her sister Maryann and the volatility of her marriage with Ray at that time. Amy was concerned about their children too. Life was hard for all of them, because of the then raging alcoholism, the continual rejections, and the constant financial problem.

You didn't know Amy was Ray's sister-in-law when you met her?

No, after we met we might have had a talk or two about it. Amy got regular phone calls from Ray and Maryann. But we were too busy just being in love those first few weeks. Then it came up that we were invited to Ray and Maryann's home in Cupertino for Christmas that year. The whole San Francisco and Stanford writers' scene was there. I met Bill Kittredge there for the first time, and Chuck Kinder and Jim Crumley.

There are quite a few stories about those Cupertino parties –

Sometimes you might find just about every important writer from the Rockies to the west and down to Santa Barbara. Lenny Michaels would be there, and Tomas Sanchez, Max Crawford, Chuck Kinder, Bill Kittredge, maybe Gurney

Norman and Ed McClanahan. It was a famous scene. Those parties would go on for weeks sometimes, moving from one place to another. The day I first met Ray was at the beginning of a long holiday party like that. I flew in ahead of Amy because of airplane ticket deals. Ray met me at the airport in a broken-down Mercury Comet station wagon full of dents and rattles and barely running. He looked like a man at the edge of death from drinking.

What year are we in?

This is December '75. Ray was waiting at the airport and he had the shakes. He could hardly wait to retrieve the bags so he could get back to the car and reach under the seat for his bottle of vodka. Then we drove up to Chuck and Diane Kinder's apartment in San Francisco and the party began. That whole Christmas was one long crazy party.

Were you meeting Ray's wife, Maryann, for the first time too?

Yes, Amy and I stayed at their home in Cupertino. It was a fun time. It was also a very rough holiday because of all the drinking. Yet Ray was so funny about that too. As soon as he got up in the morning, everyone in the house had to get up to keep him company. He'd knock on the door and shout, "Hot doughnuts! Steaming hot coffee! Come on! How about a little heart starter? Let's all just have a heart starter here!" And he'd have Bloody Marys and coffee and doughnuts along with plates of food out on the table. He'd get everybody up. We'd all tie into our drinks and be off and running again. It was a wild time.

Did you get a chance to talk to him about writing while all this was going on?

I talked to him some about writing. But writing was the last thing he wanted to talk about with a young writer from Iowa. I think he met me fully expecting to dislike me and any of the academic chichi he thought I represented.

Did he consider you an upstart?

No, but I think he expected me to be an upstart. And don't forget I was a young guy invading his home, in love with his sister-in-law, whom he loved a great deal. But we actually grew very close over the holidays. I met his brother James, and his mother, Ella, and his children, Chris and Vance. It was a good Christmas for the kids, generally. Ray played Santa Claus. Amy's daughter – our daughter – Erin, called him Uncle Ray too. Along with all the good times, I later helped Ray intervene in a difficult family situation that involved his daughter. And he stood up for me in a drunken fight, in his living room, with one of Amy's former boyfriends. We spent three weeks together, all of us partying hard, or just telling stories and jokes and mainly laughing. It was a rough time but it was also a very good time. We simply lived through so much together that by the end of the holiday we were close friends.

Do you remember what you and Ray talked about mostly?

We talked about people. His friends. Family matters. Day-to-day things. And we talked a lot about books. He only talked a little bit about his own writing. At that time he had the galleys of *Will You Please Be Quiet, Please?* Gordon Lish had gone from *Esquire* to McGraw-Hill, and I believe one of the conditions of his accepting the job as editor was that he would bring Ray's book with him and publish it there. So Ray did have that book finally on its way to being published. But to him, I think he felt this was happening way too late.

You'd think he'd be elated. What was the problem?

He was proud of the book, sure, but in a lot of ways he was also very, very grim. I remember his house in Cupertino had a lemon tree out back that was profuse with fruit that no one ever picked or tended. And Ray's study was like that tree. Books and manuscripts and papers piled up and collecting dust. He hadn't been able to work for a long time. There was so much chaos and turmoil going on in his personal life, fueled by all the drinking, that it was impossible for him to go on.

How did they manage? Who paid the bills?

Maryann was teaching English at the high school in Los Altos, where she'd worked for eight years. She had always worked. More than Ray, she paid the bills and supported the family and did everything else. But ends just didn't meet in that house. Ray at that point was hanging paper all over town, writing hot checks just to get enough liquor to get through the day.

Did he go into bankruptcy? He often wrote about it.
This was his second bankruptcy. Those stories are based on actual incidents that happened to him. In fact, I can think of only two or three stories he wrote that were not in some way based on incidents in his own life or in his own family.

Which are?
One is "The Train," which is a continuation of and an homage to a John Cheever story. Another is "Errand," his last story. But generally, I think his stories have at their core, and as points of departure, actual incidents he came across in his life.

Well, there's his story "The Pheasant." It's hard to see Ray in that story of a Hollywood bit actor, a sort of gigolo, in that car with the aging actress. Where did he get that?
He used things from everyone, things that he heard. Amy was an actress, a pro who had been on Broadway, and told him many stories. In fact, during this whole Christmas party, it was amazing to me as a young writer to sit at the table with Bill Kittredge and Ray and Chuck Kinder and the others and hear them telling stories on each other and topping each other. Ray would ask, "Are you going to use that one? Because if you're not, it's mine." And they all went around the table that way.

But Ray wasn't writing at that time.
No, but he still told great stories. The not working, and all the drinking, and the holidays were very hard on Ray and Maryann financially and every other way. Toward the end of Christmas, it was like a burnout, especially for Maryann, who had to be back at her job, paying bills and putting food on the table. Ray was in very bad shape by then.

Donald Justice

I didn't realize, and I'm not sure anyone did, how good he was going to be. Have you come across anyone who in '72 knew how successful he would become?

Of course looking back, it should have been easy to foresee. Did you meet him after '72?

Yes, he came back to teach here two or three times, and I spent some time with him at the writers' conference at Southern Methodist in '76 or '77 along with Richard Ford and Tess Gallagher, among others. I remember an afternoon in his hotel room at the end of the conference when everyone was having a good time sitting around and relaxed with Ray in his element.

Then again in '78 when he was teaching here, he and Maryann and as it turned out Doug Unger and his wife all house-sat for us while we were away for a month or so.

How did you come to choose Ray and Maryann as your housesitters?

I believe it may be that I had heard they were on the move and didn't have a place to stay, something like that. As a matter of fact, after we came back and relieved them of their duties, we called on them and they were at some other house they were sitting in for a friend. They must have been doing that for some time.

He didn't stay at Iowa much longer. Did you see him after that?

The last time I saw Ray would have been at Yaddo in the summer of 1981. By this time he had pretty much come into his own, although my impression is that the world wasn't aware of his presence as much as it would be in another year or so. It was an important year for him, a turning point. *Cathedral* had come out while we were at Yaddo, and he gave me an offprint of the book.

How do you view his work?

Well, a couple of things right off. I've read all of his poems, and I believe all of his stories. He's a real artist, which I very much appreciate, and he has a very strong sense of humanity. That is the easiest way I can put that. He has great human sympathy, which I don't believe all writers have, and I am of the opinion all writers should have it. He has it automatically, just generously from the spirit. Those are the two aspects of his artistry in particular I admire, especially as they go together.

Artistry. Could you elaborate?

His stories are *(pause)* conscientiously and idiosyncratically put together. They have a form to them, and he has a style of his own too that is as far as I can tell without pretension. It also possesses all sorts of virtues I appreciate. It is quite clear, direct, and fairly subtle. He seems to be concerned with the truth. All this may seem obvious, but it can't be said of most writers. The classical virtues exist in his best work.

But he wrote for years without recognition despite the virtues of this clear idiosyncratic style.

I have perhaps peculiar ideas on this matter that may relate to my views on poetry too. I think it is easier to spot real or even false originality in an experimental style than in a classical style. I see Ray's work in the classical style. It's not flashy or pretentious. I think a great deal of the work that has gained immediate attention in America since the Second World War has been flashy and pretentious. So Ray's work would somehow have been out of it in that way. It's astonishing that the beauty in his work did become appreciated because he didn't make compromises with the prevailing trends.

What do you think of his poetry?

I believe he was more a story writer. Almost everyone would agree to that, but I enjoy reading his poems, almost for the same reasons I like his fiction, but for me there is not so much a sense of a form being achieved or an individual style being found. I did a blurb for one of his collections, *At Night the Salmon Move*. My favorite in that book was a really funny poem about Bukowski. It is a masterpiece of comedy.

Hilarious. That poem is also in his collection Fires. *What did you think of it as poetry?*

Well, it's better than any others I can think of of its kind.

It's not, you know, the highest art but it is a great piece of comedy. I don't care whether it's poetry or prose at that point. It's poetry if it insists on having a rhythm based on speech, or variations on it. It has a comic form that he invents as he goes along, a certain improvisation.

I find a note of sadness in that poem. You can't help feeling sorry for Bukowski.

Well, I don't. I don't like his writing and I don't like his character and I don't feel the least bit sad about the man. No doubt the poem itself has more sympathy than I want to read in there. On the other hand, it's a terrific parody, and if you're a true Bukowski fan and want him to be idolized, you're not going to like the poem.

Then overall, do you find his poetry too similar to his fiction?

The poems are of a piece with the rest of his work. Let's just say he is a more finished artist in his fiction. He has more room to get people involved with one another which is one of his strengths. I was reading one of his earlier stories last night, "The Student's Wife." I particularly like those earlier stories. They strike me as having a true Chekhovian shape and form along with sympathy for characters that you wouldn't expect to be sympathetic with. That's one of the marks of Chekhov as far as I'm concerned.

That sympathy you mention – one of those earlier titles was "Put Yourself in My Shoes."

Exactly. And that sympathy would come out in a surprising way. Anybody knows it could be done in a story, and could perhaps force it, but in Ray's work it comes out naturally. You did tell me earlier that his obituary in the *London Times* described him as the American Chekhov. I wonder if there is an English Chekhov.

That sounds like a contradiction in terms.

In Ray's stories you can see the way they come directly from experience, but at the same time you don't feel the same way as you often do when the writing is more or less autobiographical as in, say, D. H. Lawrence's *Sons and Lovers*. You don't feel the same kind of terrible egoism. Carver was able to use himself and his own experience, but in a more objective way. He was in his stories, but he also saw it, and from a distance, and I think that's a great benefit in his stories. I sometimes wonder if you can see Ray's friends in those stories. I know you can often see Maryann, as in all those stories where the main characters are the husband and the wife.

As in perhaps the story you mentioned earlier, "The Student's Wife"?

The truth is I don't know that much about the actual circumstances of Ray's life, but what one knows from a distance seems reflected, even recorded in those stories. It strikes me especially in those stories about husband and wife who aren't getting along but who seem to be still in love. There's a kind of built-in terrible tension in the husband and wife pairs which I've always easily associated with his marriage to Maryann. Again, not that I had any particular insights or knowledge of it, but what one did sense from the outside, there did seem to be that kind of character to the relationship. And of course if that was so, it turned out to be a rich mine of fiction for him. Could hardly have been better.

Chuck Kinder

Ray always said that you should trust the accidents in your work, and of course in your life. In "Are You a Doctor?" suddenly there's a random telephone call – there are so many phone calls in Ray's work. Out of the blue, a sudden telephone call that sets off a series of events that then take on mysterious meaning. You don't know exactly what they mean, that's the mystery.

The interview takes place in the kitchen of the sixteen-room, turn-of-the-century, yellow brick house in Pittsburgh where Chuck Kinder lives with his wife, Diane. Chuck always holds his long, serious conversations over kitchen tables wherever he lives. It comes from a warm, old-fashioned, country way of living. After the interview, I sit in on the writing class he teaches at the University of Pittsburgh and learn a thing or two about the art of fiction from this good ol' country boy.

Would you describe your first meeting with Ray?

I don't remember when I first met him, but I know when he first made an impression on me. It was in '72, when we were at Stanford together. He had a Stegner fellowship and I had an Edith Mirrelees fellowship, and I must have met him the first day in workshop, but I don't remember. I'd seen him sitting around mumbling a lot, and smoking, and biting on his thumbnail. He'd make comments now and then on the other students' stories, not a lot of comments, but when he did, they were really astute. I was impressed with that.

How old was he then?

Oh, about thirty-four. He was a big shambling fellow, always wore shades. I thought he dressed goofy. He looked like someone who I'd take their lunch money away from when I was a kid. At any rate, one day I needed a ride down El Camino Real and I asked if anyone was going in that direction. Ray raised his hand and said he was going in that direction, and I said to myself, Dear God, not this goofy guy.

Had you been avoiding him all this time?

Well, not exactly. You have to understand that those were the days when *The Whole Earth Catalog* was current. It was hip to be close to the earth and all that. Everyone was walking around wearing work boots and work clothes, and since I came from West Virginia and I'd worked in a coal mine, I could affect that look with a little more authority.

And what was Ray wearing?

He looked like a big goofball. Corduroy pants. Shirts that he had buttoned up to the collar. Like he didn't care if he was cool at all. He looked like no one who'd interest me. And of course it turned out later that was wonderful, that he didn't think about bullshit like that. Anyway, I took him up on his offer of a ride and we went out to the parking lot. He had an old battered Mercury convertible that looked like it would fall apart, even while we looked at it. Someone had dumped the ashtray all over the car floor. That car was full of crap – manuscripts, paper cups, cigarette butts everywhere.

And a load of unpaid parking tickets?

Oh sure, all that. Then we had to pray that the car would start. It coughed, and hacked, and wheezed, and bounced all over the lot. About that time a bottle slid out from under the seat, a bottle of very cheap scotch. And Ray looked down at it and said, "Ooh, look what we have here," laughing in that way of his. "How do you suppose this got here? Maybe we should have us a little drink. What do you think?" So I said, "Sure, why not? Let's have us a little drink." And he passed it over. I don't know what scotch it was. It tasted like hair tonic. It was about a half a quart, and he didn't have far to take me, just three miles down El Camino, but we pretty near killed it by the time he let me off. I thought this guy was a nut, and I didn't want him to know where I lived on Matadora Road, so I told him to let me off at the corner at the Taco Bell. He did, and he drove off in that old car bouncing into the sunset looking like an accident waiting to happen. And I thought that was the last time I'm going to have anything to do with him. It wasn't that I disliked the guy, it's just that I couldn't figure him out.

Sounds like you took him for a nerd.

Yeah, he was a nerd. He wasn't a hip, red-necked good ol' boy like me at all.

Well, we know he wasn't a nerd, and that it wasn't the last you saw of him. When did you see him next?

My first wife, Janet, and I lived in a little bungalow we rented from a woman whose father had built it by hand. She gave us a break on the rent for me to do the yardwork, which I never did. When she'd come to check things out, I'd be hiding inside with the curtains drawn and wouldn't answer the door. Well, about ten o'clock the next morning, I heard a pounding on the door, and I thought it was the landlady. I got very quiet and turned off the TV, but the knocking kept on. Rap, rap, rap, and finally I took a peek, and it was Ray with a pile of magazines and books in one arm and a bag in the other arm.

What was in the bag?

More magazines and a bottle of cheap booze and some ice. These were magazines he had stories in. At that time he had eight or nine stories published in magazines like *Quarterly West* and other small magazines. There he was, and I let him in.

There he was. Did he just want to hang out with you?

Yeah, he asked me if I was working on anything. And I told him to get serious, I was only watching TV. So we went out to the kitchen, sat down, had a drink, and started talking. He gave me copies of his stories he wanted me to read. I was pleased at that. I gave him a copy of my first novel that had just come out. I had finished it after my first year at Stanford and thought I was pretty much of a hotshot. That may have been another reason I'd been snotty to him.

What was your reaction to his work after you read it?

I was amazed by it. I thought it was wonderful writing. It was spare, but what really impressed me then, as it continues to impress me now, is – I don't want to get into all this analysis of his work –

I'm sorry, Chuck, but I'm afraid you may have to.

Well, what I liked then, and what I keep returning to now, and what I talk about to my classes – we always go over two or three of his stories every term, and always "Cathedral" because it epitomizes one of the things I really care about in writing – and that is the discovery of the mystery in the mundane. He could find the art in everyday occurrences. I read somewhere that early Christianity had such appeal because it made mystery democratic. It wasn't filtered down through priests. You could have mystery in your everyday life. In an amazing way, Ray did that with his work, in that strange conjunction between accident and art.

Did you recognize this in his work from the start?

Yes, especially in stories like "Are You a Doctor?" and "Put Yourself in My Shoes," those stories. I liked the Kafkaesque quality in those stories, the way accidents happen that can determine your fate. Ray always said that you should trust the accidents in your work, and of course in your life. In "Are

37

You a Doctor?" suddenly there's a random telephone call –
there are so many phone calls in Ray's work. Out of the blue, a
sudden telephone call that sets off a series of events that then
take on mysterious meaning. You don't know exactly what they
mean, that's the mystery. You have to read Ray's work with the
same intensity as you read poetry. Those stories, to my mind,
sort of pointed toward what Flannery O'Connor talks about as
a big mystery. The big mystery beneath the surface of the
story. Especially in Ray's stories that had a mystery, there's a
sense of a crafted meaning that glimmered under the surface
of the story. At any rate, I always thought the title of his first
collection should have been *Put Yourself in My Shoes*, but Gordon Lish insisted on *Will You Please Be Quiet, Please?*, which
is a wonderful story, of course, and that's the way it went.

*Let's go back to what happened after Ray's first visit to
you back in Stanford.*

Well, we started hanging out together, and a couple of
nights later he brought Maryann over to meet my wife. We
never actually did talk that much about writing, thank God.
We'd be sitting around talking about events in our lives, and it
would be interesting to see how he and Maryann would talk
about horrific things they had gone through. Bill Kittredge has
a terrific story about a couple of old funky barroom ladies who
have learned to cut their losses to jokes. And that's what happened with Ray and Maryann. They'd tell these horrific stories
and they'd be laughing about them. The stories took on a legendary tall tale quality, and they'd embellish them as they
went along.

It's interesting that when Ray was drinking, he'd blank out
a lot. His memory would be affected, and Maryann's wasn't. So
very often Ray would question her, almost like an interview,
asking, "Then what did I do after that?" I could see the story
taking root in Ray's mind as Maryann would plumb her memory about events. That happened time and time again. So when
you were with them, there was a sense of play, dangerous play
true, that they were amazed by and always trying to understand. But with all that booze, it got dark and evil toward the
end, really destructive, and Ray couldn't handle it.

We're told there may be a genetic factor to alcoholism.

Oh yes. Ray's father was an alcoholic. Alcohol acted as a sort of fuel for him. And of course he was basically very shy. It was interesting that so many of the things they did that make up all the Ray and Maryann stories and anecdotes, I could see them being created, not consciously I'm sure, but as though they were trying to create a story to tell later. An accident would happen that would lead to another, and he would trust the accidents and sort of follow where they led, each moment having its own fan-shaped destiny. There was a certain child-like quality to all that, a strange sense of play. You'll see kids fighting and saying, I hate you, I hate you. Then a few minutes later, they're best friends again. We'd have situations when there'd be a shattering of glass, and yells and screams, and howls in the night, and the next minute they'd be ordering pizza. And then Maryann would say, "Did you see what Ray just did?" and then tell the story as if it were all some kind of amazing game whose rules they were trying to discover after the fact. There was a hilarity to it, but that ultimately feeds on itself. The fiction devours itself.

Was all this while you were still at Stanford, in Palo Alto?

Yes, but they were living in Cupertino. As I said, my first wife and I and Ray and Maryann started running together. I remember one night we had to carry them home and literally put them in bed. Maryann was so impressed by that. She laughed and said their other friends would just dump them on the porch for their kids to find them in the morning.

Could you tell more about how they reacted to each other?

Sure. It was on their fifteenth or sixteenth wedding anniversary. Maryann was amazingly generous. Ray was generous too, but when it came to money, he could be a little tight. Ray and I had this relationship where we'd bicker a lot. You know, one-upmanship, like bickering brothers. Like did you buy that last drink, or did I buy the last two, and all that business. Maryann, though, with her last penny would buy a turkey or a ham and throw a party for the whole neighborhood.

So they came sweeping over to my house, they'd had a few and were real high and funny. She invited Janet and me to go out and celebrate with them at a Greek restaurant. When we got there, Ray got upset with her. Obviously she had been to this restaurant before, and she wouldn't come clean as to who she'd been there with or why, and he was very suspicious. But at that point, Ray was involved with someone else, and Maryann was at the edges of some stuff also. So there was suspicion between the both of them. So we all were at this Greek restaurant, and it turned into a typical Carver story.

I remember they had a floor show, and they had a strongman who picked up tables with his teeth. At one point he did a backbend and invited people from the audience to come up and step on his stomach. His assistant took Ray by the hand and pulled him up there. Ray was laughing and saying OK, OK. He stumbled and tumbled all over that strongman. One crazy thing after another. But as the evening wore on, Ray decided since he was paying for it, that he couldn't afford any more. I was pegged out but kept ordering more drinks, more champagne. Ray was getting more irritated with me. He started sulking, saying we're not paying for him. After awhile he decided that we'd walk the check. My wife had seen and heard enough. She was a real sweet, straight arrow and had seen enough of our silly act. She went out to the car to wait for us to settle the whole thing. She was the designated driver, and we were the designated drunks all the time. The next thing I knew Ray had disappeared. He was going to stick me with the check. I told Maryann that I had no money, no plastic, nothing. She had some plastic, but on more than a few occasions in the past, their card had come back, a pitiful thing, cut in two on a tray, rejected. Maryann wasn't sure whether the plastic she had was good or not, so she told me to go out through the bar, and she would walk out slowly later. We were going to walk the check after all.

When I got out to the car, my wife was behind the wheel, engine going, and Ray was lying low, lurking in the back seat. Then Maryann came out, and just then our waiter came out and put his hand on Maryann's shoulder. Ray said to my wife,

"Step on it, step on it!" He wanted to leave Maryann behind in the dust, anniversary or no anniversary. I talked some sense back into him. We went back into the restaurant, and Maryann was sitting at the bar giving the cashier her plastic. Ray was worried, asking her what they were going to do if it wasn't any good. Maryann said that she would then have to write them a check, which was a laugh. She had all the bravado in the world, and she could carry it off. She really had a flair. The plastic worked, thank God, and we got out of there.

After his year at Stanford, did he go up to Berkeley?

Yes, Lenny Michaels got him in there. Once, Ray got me fifty bucks for reading to his class, and we drank it up at a hotel bar in Berkeley ahead of time. He wanted me to meet a girl in his class who had written a story about being gang-banged by a biker club. She had a crush on Ray, and he was frightened to death of her. He wanted me to meet her. She was a cute tattooed chick. He introduced me to the class first as a panel, then as Truman Capote. We ended by driving up to Davis to see Jack Hicks, stopping at a bar on the way called Dutch's. One thing leads to another, and the alcohol acts as a fuel, and you could see the story happening. Nothing really happened with the girl. Well, not much. But it got on the verge of crazy stuff. At one point we both decided we were in love with her. Anyway, we were living the story, and knowing we were living it, first making it into a literary tall tale, and then making it into a one-upmanship story that we would tell at a kitchen table. We spent a lot of time at kitchen tables batting stories back and forth, until the truth was just where we wanted it to be.

How long did he stay at Berkeley, and why did he leave?

He was teaching at Berkeley while he had his Stegner at Stanford. You weren't supposed to do that, but he was always pulling stunts like that. He'd send his stories out to half a dozen magazines at once. That story, "So Much Water So Close to Home," was published in two separate journals before he sold it to *Playgirl*.

Did he make any revisions before he sent it out?

No, no, the same story.

*Was it right about then that he worked up that deal
where he was teaching at Iowa and Santa Cruz at the
same time?*

Yes, that's when he would teach at Iowa the beginning of
the week and fly back to Santa Cruz to teach at the end of the
week. That's when I met Bill Kittredge, who was down at
Stanford on a Stegner. I don't know how many times Bill and I
went up to teach Ray's class at Santa Cruz.

He sort of pulled this again later when he was teaching at
Santa Barbara. Only that time he was collecting unemployment checks from the state while he was working. He almost
went to jail on that one, but Maryann saved his bacon. She got
up in court and pled everything but her belly to get him on
probation. It took Maryann, Kittredge, Max Crawford, and
myself all to drag Ray down for the first meeting with his probation officer. We had to literally walk him to the door and
shove him in.

*Was this when you and your wife were still running
around with Ray and Maryann?*

No, this was later. My first wife and I had split up by
then. I had been on leave from Stanford, where I was by then a
Jones lecturer, when my first wife justifiably parked me at the
curb, and I had nowhere to go, so Bill Kittredge offered me
a little spot up in Missoula. Ray and Maryann were having
trouble, because he was deeply in love with another woman
whom he had been involved with for a couple of years. Maryann had found a pack of letters from this woman, so Ray gave
me some stuff to take back for safekeeping to this woman
when I went back to Montana to live with Bill. That's where
this woman lived. I met her and gave her the stuff from Ray.
That was Diane, my present wife. I fell madly in love with her.
I felt bad about Ray, but he had his chance. He had broken
promises with her for years. He hadn't left Maryann and it
looked like he never would. When Kittredge went back to
Stanford and told Ray, he said that Ray was real pissed at me.
Ray said that we always called him Running Dog, but Kinder
was the real running dog.

How did you make up?

Ray phoned one day and we talked it all over, and when the conversation was over, we were laughing. He was calling me names like back-stabber and asshole and all that. You'd think it would affect our friendship, but it didn't. When Diane and I moved back down to Palo Alto before we moved to San Francisco, Ray had moved back in with Maryann, and we all went out together, and we were closer as couples than we had been when I was married to my first wife.

A good friend, Scott Turow, who was at Stanford with us also was heading back east with his wife, Annette, and they had a great flat in San Francisco. Their landlord lived right above them and was a real asshole. Scott figured that the way to get even with the landlord was to let me have the flat when he left. Scott knew I'd drive that landlord nuts, and that's exactly what we did. Ray and Maryann would come up every weekend, and it was a continuous party. It was amazing the people who would hang out up there. People like S. Clay Wilson, the cartoonist, and some Hawaiian gangsters I had met when I first came to San Francisco. Ray was fascinated by these guys, who would lay their guns out on the table. These were real serious guys.

Aren't we getting close to the time now when Ray started to make some attempts to quit drinking?

Well, this is the story I told Tess for the first time just last week when she was here for a visit. It was the first time I felt truly that Ray and Maryann would break up, that it would really happen. Maryann had started to go to AA and she had become involved with someone down there, and back when Maryann had found out about Diane and Ray, she had gone off and had a brief fling with someone else and told Ray about it, and they had gone a couple of rounds over it. So there was a history of violence.

But now they were back together again and over at our place one weekend before going off for a week of fishing. Maryann was dressed up in a beautiful white dress for dinner. They were talking about the future and waxing nostalgic about the past, but there was a lot of tension going on as the drinking got heavier and heavier. Maryann was trying to keep it afloat, being witty and lively, but I could sense Ray was in a lot of pain. He could become very jealous at times, and when the rage and pain would come from so deep within him, it would frighten him to death, and he was leery of it.

Just about then Shorty Ramos, one of the Hawaiian gangsters, showed up, and, trying to goad Ray, Maryann started flirting with Shorty. There were a couple of kisses at the table, and things were building up. Then Shorty left and I went to bed, thinking things would cool down. Maryann and Ray were sitting on the couch, and my wife, Diane, was sitting across from them. She was just sitting there watching them drink and fight. Diane said you could see the intensity mounting. Then they both stood up, and Maryann said something to Ray, and he hit her on the side of her head with a bottle, and the bottle shattered, glass flying across the room. Maryann ran out of the house and just disappeared. Diane and Ray went out after her. Diane told him to go back in the house and stay there, and he did. Diane then followed a trail of blood and found Maryann standing in an alley, dazed and bleeding profusely. Diane led her back to the house. I woke up when I felt someone squeezing my foot. It was Maryann, and her white dress was drenched in blood. She said, "Look what Ray did."

I jumped up and got a towel and pressed it to her neck. Diane called for an ambulance, and they took her to the hospital, Diane going with her. Ray and I sat out at the kitchen table, but he couldn't talk. He was devastated by what he had done.

Had you not acted so quickly, Maryann could have died, and Ray would have gone to prison. Talk about trusting your accidents. That changed their lives, but it could have been tragic.

No question about it. She would have bled to death. But it was Diane who saved her life. This was as violent as it ever got. There had been black eyes and such, but nothing like this. And after those violent events, there was always such a tenderness between them that was hard to explain. He moved in to stay with us, and Maryann came over after she had been discharged from the hospital. He was sitting there smoking, shamefaced, and you could see the pain in his eyes. Maryann went over to him and placed her hands on the back of his head and gently patted him. She didn't say much. A friend came and picked her up, and she went to stay with her friend.

It's hard to believe they'd ever get back together after this incident, but they did, didn't they?

Yes, a number of times. Funny thing, he couldn't remember hitting her with the bottle. Even years later, after he stopped drinking and we'd get together or talk over the phone, he had no memory of it. On occasion he would ask me questions about that night and all that had happened, who did what and when. I can remember him shaking his old woolly head and saying very Carverish things like, who was that person? Who was that person who said he was me? Who was that person using my name? Those were very strange times. I remember once when we were all out at Ocean Beach, and the body of a drowned man washed up not fifty feet from where we had spread our blankets. Really, this actually happened. Diane spotted him first. His eyes were open and fixed. He was a guy of about thirty-five, muscular and handsome, and he had all these tattoos on his arms. Ray and I began bickering on what to do, about who should try to give the poor devil mouth to mouth or something, but neither of us moved a muscle. Ray suggested there was a phone in the Beach Chalet bar across the road he could use for help. Sure, Ray. Finally, a man in a red wetsuit tried to give him mouth to mouth, for all the good it did. Anyway, later that day Ray and I decided what we needed to do for ourselves was get tattoos. So we sat at the kitchen table for hours drinking and drawing tattoo designs. That whatever I drew, Ray would have inked on his skin, and vice-versa. I drew something I wanted to look like both a valentine heart and a skull, and I wrote DIANE across it. Then Ray drew a pretty good picture of a real heart, an anatomical heart, not some valentine heart, and he wrote MARYANN in it. Crazy.

Anyway, they kept separating and getting together, and for a while they had a sweet little attic apartment on Castro that Maryann fixed up, as only Maryann can. It was a sweet time for them, maybe the last sweet time. Maryann was going to AA, but Ray was still drinking seriously and in and out of hospitals. He had collapsed in a doctor's office. They gave him several stitches and said he had wet brain. He went up to Duffy's, and Maryann went seriously into AA. And that was when she met a guy there who appears in a couple of Ray's stories.

Is this Ross of "Mr. Coffee and Mr. Fixit"?
Yep, that's him.

Was he an engineer?
Well, he said he was, I guess. First I heard he was an astronaut. Then he was a big rocket engineer. Then it kept getting lower and lower.

Just like Mr. Fixit. Ray says in the story that he had his number when he saw two busted Plymouths in the guy's yard.
Well, Maryann was involved with that guy. She'd go down to see him, and that was upsetting to Ray. They were having an anniversary or something, and Ray had bought champagne and flowers, and then she didn't show up. She comes back two or three hours later, and there's Ray at the top of the stairs with all the flowers torn and ripped up all around him.

That sounds like the kernel for "A Serious Talk."
Could be. They used to go down to Market Street and spend afternoons watching porn movies. They'd have their sweet times together, but it was the last of the sweet times. There were a lot of breakups. Ray went to Duffy's again, and Doug, Amy, and I went to pick him up in Doug's little old red Toyota truck. On the way back, Ray and I rode in the back, bouncing around like a pair of field hands in the bed of that truck, because Doug drove like a maniac. We talked a lot, smoking some dope. Ray smoked dope all his life. He never did quit that. He told me he thought he was real close to having his last drink. And he talked about his father and how his father died, most of which I'd heard before, but not told with such emotion and sadness. When it had happened, his mother called Maryann and told her out of the blue, that Ray was dead. It took awhile for Maryann to realize she was talking about Ray's

father, who was also called Ray. Ray talked a whole lot about his father. It was a sad trip back, but by the time we hit the Golden Gate Bridge, we were laughing again.

You were talking about the last of their sweet times. Ray wrote a story, "Chef's House," describing their last sweet time together. Could you tell us something about that?

I was coming back with Diane from giving a reading at the writers' conference in Port Townsend, and we stopped to visit them at Chef's house. That was a real sweet time. Neither of them were drinking, but it was a sad time. There was a sense of loss. Another time Diane had received a little money from an inheritance. She wanted to throw a party of course, so she sent Ray money for round-trip airfare from Iowa City, where he was living then. He bought a one-way ticket, and he used the leftover money to drive Maryann back with him to Iowa.

Didn't he then leave Iowa for El Paso? That must have been their last breakup. What do you know about that?

They had all kinds of problems in Iowa, too much emotional baggage, and that was really the end of their time together. Ray later told me it was Maryann who set him adrift. They had a mournful but loving talk deciding what to do. He had the teaching job lined up in El Paso, and she had some money coming from her teachers' retirement fund. So she was the one who actually said it, "You go off and have a good life in El Paso, I'm going to California." She made the decision. He got into this old car that his son, Vance, had left there and drove off for El Paso. And that pretty much was the end of it. Of course the car broke down on the way.

Wasn't that where he met Tess again, in El Paso?

Yes, she was a reinforcement in his life, a real steadying influence. She's a strong woman, a class act. Maryann went back to California, and I can't remember the last time I saw her. She cut herself off from all their old friends. Al Young ran into her in a drugstore in Palo Alto many years ago, and she was distant and obviously didn't want to talk. It was her decision to remove herself from our lives, although we still have so much affection for her.

Scott Turow

There's a massive difference between the writer as a person on the one hand and his work on the other. There's an invisible element in writers. Indeed, one of the things that drove me to law school was the fact that hanging around with these guys, I came to realize that writers as a group do a miserable job of talking about themselves. They'd be happy to tell you stories, repeat stories to you that they heard, but when it came to talking about their inner selves . . . very little. I found that lawyers are much more open . . . Writers in many ways write because there are things that are otherwise unapproachable for them.

The interview takes place up on the eightieth floor of Chicago's Sears Tower. We are in the conference room of the prominent law firm where novelist Turow becomes attorney Turow after 2 P.M. each working day. He apologizes for interruptions as he takes care of matters that just can't wait, though there is no denying his alert interest and commitment to the interview. He is a professional.

When we were talking about Carver earlier, you referred to the Beef Trust. Could you tell me more about that?

That's how I used to refer to Kinder, Kittredge, and Carver. They were an imposing looking group, slightly reminiscent of last year's Phillies. They didn't look a bit like writers – more like truck drivers. They'd come striding across the quad at Stanford elbow to elbow looking purposeful, if not mean. They were physically impressive – all heavy. They were all drinking hard in those years.

When was this?

Oh, this was around 1975. The three of them were really interested in each other, which made plenty of sense because they were a little older than most of the other writing Fellows, but more to the point, they had each thought an enormous amount about fiction, the purposes of narrative, what it could accomplish and how it did it. They were interested in each other at a very serious intellectual level, plus they favored the same forms of entertainment, and the three of them shared an extremely dark sense of humor.

What was Carver's position at Stanford then?

I don't really know. I recently got into some debates with people at Stanford as to when exactly Ray showed up. My recollection is that Ray was a writing Fellow at Stanford in 1973 to '74 or maybe '74 to '75. I may be wrong. I was in the workshop from '70 to '72 and started teaching in the fall of '72 and Ray appeared shortly after that as a writing Fellow. If my memory is right, he had just come from Iowa. In time he became a commanding force at the writing center.

Commanding force?

Well, Ray at that point had been at Iowa and even had taught for a while. He was not an average student in the class. He was older and more developed, both as a writer and in his ability to talk about writing.

Hadn't some of his stories and poems been published by then?

I think so. I remember stories of his being published while he was at Stanford.

How close did you get to Ray? Did you know Maryann?

I saw Ray and Maryann at parties and social functions, but it wasn't an intimate friendship, certainly nothing remotely like his closeness with Kittredge or Kinder. I knew Ray at a distance and found him in a way somewhat intimidating. As for Maryann, when I saw her, frankly most of the time we were all drinking. She was very nice. I enjoyed her company. She was humorous and always kind to me.

How would you describe Ray and Maryann together?

From my limited observation, they had a rather destructive relationship, but it was also intimate and full of appreciation for each other. Ray had a lot of respect for Maryann, but there were legendary stories about their physical cruelty to each other. One I heard in Ray and Maryann's presence was about them driving down a mountain road together, coming back from Santa Cruz, winding their way on Route 84 and trying to burn each other with cigarettes. The car nearly went off the road with all the cat fighting and howling. They were laughing about it afterwards.

Just a couple of wild and crazy kids, right?

The thing that must be said about Maryann is that in all my dealings with her, she was a genuinely kind person – open and funny, complex, and to me in my early twenties probably even inscrutable.

What else did you see in Ray at this time?
Well, there was a very bleak side to him.

Would you attribute that to the booze or to the general nature of the man?
I don't know. I didn't know him sober.

How do you see that bleak side in his stories?
You get the sense of Ray from the stories that he was willing to embrace the cruelty of life in people with a little more mettle than most of us, and that he could therefore accept his own cruelty. One of the things I found intimidating about the Kinder-Kittredge-Carver crew when they were together was not that they were ever mean to anybody else. That's not the way they operated. There was nothing hostile; they were fun to be around. You didn't have to worry about them beating you with a pool cue, but they took a level of merriment about cruel things as in the Carver story about the father driving off to abandon the family dog and then telling the kids it was lost. That was the kind of thing that in my midtwenties I was not yet able to accept. It was kind of threatening to deal with people whose view of the world was that dark.

Black humor, gallows humor? That was in his work.
What I'm talking about is accepting negative human capacity without sentimentality on the one hand or glorification on the other. The question – the moral, ethical question – is, do you expect less of yourself when you accept that? That, of course, is an issue that the people who were closest to Ray would have to decide. I have no way of knowing that.

Well, do you believe whatever dilemma this presented to Ray was translated into his stories?
Yes, but there is a massive difference between the writer as a person on the one hand and his work on the other. There's

an invisible element in writers. Indeed, one of the things that drove me to law school was the fact that hanging around with these guys, I came to realize that writers as a group do a miserable job of talking about themselves. They'd be happy to tell you stories, repeat stories to you that they heard, but when it came to talking about their inner selves . . . very little. I found that lawyers are much more open in some ways, even if the inner world is not always as rich. Writers in many ways write because there are things that are otherwise unapproachable for them. Again, I was not one of Ray's intimates, but I'd say Ray was one of those writers who, when he was talking, didn't really share personal experience except the fabulous tales about himself, the ones that were repeated around him. The wild stories like the sixteen year old saying "Shut up, Dad. You're drunk," or Ray falling asleep drunk in the driveway. Stuff like that was always repeated around him because it happened, and he'd laugh about it as the tales were told.

Getting away from that – did you follow his career after you went on your way to law school?

Yes, I continued to read his stories as they appeared in the magazines and his books as they came out. I liked his work a great deal.

And you continued your own writing?

I didn't give up writing. I gave up living in a literary community.

And though you're a busy, active attorney, you are still a writer.

God willing, I certainly feel I am. Whether I am, I leave to the judgment of others. You meet me here in my law office and I live principally in a community of lawyers, but one of the things I've discovered is you don't have to live with writers to be a writer. You know places like Stanford or Iowa have a lot of romance attached to them, and people come hoping that something is going to rub off on them, that somehow the company of other writers, and the drinking, the carousing, the running around, is going to make them "literary." Maybe it does. It wasn't working for me.

So you left teaching at Stanford to attend law school?

I went to law school. I didn't relish academic life. I'm not sure Ray did either. Teaching was a way for a writer to make a living. I didn't particularly regard myself as a scholar. Kittredge was a scholar. He enjoyed studying for the sake of studying, beyond what it fueled in his own imagination.

What were you writing at that time?

I was writing realistic fiction with strong plot lines – same as always. I admired the abstract and theoretical, but what came out of me was meat and potatoes. I was writing a lot of short stories at the time, odd slices of middle-class life, but nothing to rival Carver's work.

Very little has been written to rival those stories. How would you assess his work?

I admire it very much. I think of it as outstanding work. To me it's defined by what we've been talking about. Much as we would understand by the term Kafkaesque, there's a sort of Carveresque view which avoids a standard response to the big or little cruelties of life. What was most original in Ray's work to my mind was that he refigured experience the way our best writers do. And he constantly portrayed characters whose reactions were at once believable but which didn't conform to the standard myths and previous literary reconstructions. Defining these reactions is tricky. There's a lot of Beckett in Ray Carver. His work is unsentimental, at times unhopeful, and unwilling to pretend that people aren't capable of these kinds of cruelties and infractions. Yet beneath it all is the wry knowledge that people are going to go on, so what's the point of denouncing all this misery since people are going to suffer it anyway and make their accommodations. No sense wringing our hands in anguish.

Or trying to draw a moral from it?

You know it would be interesting to learn what Ray would think of the lawyer's life. If we could sit him on the bench and say, "OK Judge Carver, now you have to declare this person guilty or not guilty, and then determine the punishment."

Can you see that? Not very likely.

No, of course not. He wasn't at all interested in those kind of judgments. He knew what every lawyer soon finds out, that those judgments are never completely correct. He understood that people are capable of a great deal, and he didn't believe in correct responses. That's what his stories exemplify again and again. That's the genius of the story "A Small Good Thing," where the baker and the parents end up together talking and talking. That was the Carveresque vision. How oddly, and in defiance of our stereotypes and myths, life really occurs.

William Kittredge

You, Kinder, and Carver were together at Stanford –

When I showed up at Stanford in September '73, the first thing Ray did was take me to a get-together at Chuck Kinder's house and it was one of those fortunate things where there were maybe ten people there and most are still friends of mine. We kept seeing each other in a tight little society of writers and drunks, and we became close friends, dear friends that I have to this day.

> *This stretch of time sounds very much like what Ray*
> *called his Bad Raymond days. Could you tell us what*
> *you know of how he got out of it?*

Well, what happened was we'd visit in San Francisco and see him at Chuck Kinder's place. Chuck had a big, spacious flat, and we'd all gather up there at spring break or Christmas. Ray told me at the time, and I mean there were lots of things I wasn't in on, but the thing that really – well, Gordon Lish came to San Francisco to visit on one of those springs and Ray comported himself in a kind of crazy fashion, and I think it was what happened on that visit that compelled him to really look at his life and say, I have to straighten up or I'm not going to last. It was at this time he made deliberate, life-saving decisions. They weren't very easy decisions. They were difficult, but the narrator in that story "Where I'm Calling From" is closely autobiographical. Ray may have embellished it some, but that was the real stuff.

Did he go to a place to dry out?

Yep. He went to McKinleyville, where he sobered up and where he lived in a little house by himself for a while. He and Maryann were separated at that time, and he told me that what he was doing there mainly was not drinking. He wasn't writing. I remember asking him after he had been sober for about six months if he had been writing at all. He said, "I can't. I can't convince myself enough that it is worth doing." That was real shaking to me. Jesus, this guy's in worse trouble than I thought. Then he slowly found his way back into it, and in a couple of years of course he was full steam again. I think those must have been extraordinarily difficult times for him. There was Dick Day, he still teaches up there I believe, who looked after him a lot while he was drying out in McKinleyville, helped him get through all that stuff.

You mentioned that small house he lived in when he left McKinleyville. Was that where he got the idea for "Chef's House"?

Must have been. When he left that house, he and Maryann came up to Montana, and we lived in a cabin on Flathead Lake for a week of fishing. Ray was a maniacal fisherman and outfished everybody. He was as singleminded about that as he was about everything else. He was *determined* to catch big fish, and more fish than anybody else, and he did. It was about this time that he and Maryann finally drifted apart. During that week they were amiable, comfortable with each other, but clearly not connected as they had been. Their relationship had broken.

Maryann Carver

Yet we'd both long before given up our personal selves for his literature. I had to lose my life to gain my life, so to speak. Looked at one way, Lenny Michaels was right. We did pay for those stories with our lives. Ray is dead, and I've lost my identity. And about that story,

"Intimacy," God bless Ray. He wrote whatever came to him, and if he could use anything, he did.

At first Maryann Carver rejected my request for a meeting. She would not discuss those personal matters over which she had maintained a steadfast silence all these years. I told her of my talk with her sister Amy when I interviewed Doug Unger, and how Bill Kittredge and Lenny Michaels had recalled her with such affectionate concern. She said she would meditate on it.

I meet with Maryann in the restored 1910 farmhouse she moved from its original site to the tract of land her grandfather had homesteaded. We are seven miles from Blaine, a border town in the northwest corner of Washington. She has converted the old house into Mariposa, home of the blue butterfly, a spiritual retreat and learning center for those seeking guidance, comfort, and transformation. I see a table covered with copies of Ray's books, snapshots, memorabilia, and scented candles. Near it is a piano with a photograph of Ray in place of the sheet music.

Maryann is introspective as she considers each question. She is exploring a lifetime of unexpressed remembrance, and she will tell it her way. We break twice so she can supervise a group practicing Reiki in the basement. Reiki, she tells me, is a Japanese word symbolizing the relationship between Universal Life Energy and our personal life force, and would I care to participate in a session. We go down to the basement, a shadowy, candle-lit room, where a dozen people seem to be meditating as they walk in slow random patterns around the room. I smell incense and hear muted Japanese music. Maryann leads me to a padded table.

I lie down and soon feel a pair of clasped hands gently elevate and support my head like a pillow. Other hands massage my feet and toes, while fingertips drum swiftly but softly up, down, and across my body. I close my eyes. I meditate on how I could have journeyed no farther in the continental U.S.A. from my house in South Miami than to this house, this table, this trip.

Can you recall the first time you saw Ray?
Oh, yes. It was in June 1955. I was almost fifteen and he

had just turned seventeen. I was working at my first real job at a place called the Spudnut Shop. It was a doughnut shop in Union Gap, Washington, a suburb of Yakima. Ray's mother was also employed there, so I knew his mother before I knew him, but I didn't know he was Ella's son. So this very good looking young man came in with his younger brother and sat down on a stool. When I first saw him I had this incredible intuition that he was going to be the father of my children. Of course I didn't know in those days about past lives and that sort of thing. I just had that immediate recognition when I saw him. We looked at each other and smiled with delight. We knew each other.

When did you and Ray marry?

It was on June 7, 1957. We went together for two years before we were married, and for most of that time I was attending a private college preparatory school for girls.

Did Ray show any desire to be a writer at that time?

Well, Ray always wanted to write. He wanted to be a writer from the third grade on.

Where did you live after you were married?

During our first year we lived in Ray's family doctor's apartment that was underneath his office. We'd clean his office in payment for rent and utilities, and he even paid for the newspaper and telephone. That was our daily job.

Did you decide that Ray should go on to college?

We had talked about that for as long as we had known each other. As I said, I had gone to a private school, comparable to a junior college. When a girl graduated from there she could go to Vassar or Wellesley or wherever. I had a scholarship from the University of Washington to study law. Ray and I had discussed all this. We wrote to each other every day while I was at school, and when I wasn't at school we saw each other every day. Then when he moved with his family to California, we kept up this incredible correspondence. I remember writing to him that I was working ten and twelve hours a day so that I could get a scholarship, and that I wouldn't be happy with anyone who didn't want to go to college.

Did Ray share your feelings about college?
No, Ray didn't want to go to college. He wanted to work and make money to buy a car, and a phonograph, and clothes and things like that. And that's exactly what he did for a year.

Were you married at the time?
No, he graduated a year ahead of me.

What was Ray doing during that year?
He worked part of the year down in California and earned the money to buy a car, the hi-fi, and some of the material things that he really lusted for. And that was more important for him at that time than to go to college. Then he missed me, and I missed him, so he came back to Washington. I was at the girls' school, so he stayed with his aunt in Yakima. He'd come down to see me at school in Walla Walla as often as the school permitted me to have a guest. Then later that year he and two friends decided that they were going to South America. He had been heavily influenced by the movie *King Solomon's Mines*, having seen it about fourteen times. He loved movies – we both did. Anyway, he wanted to pick diamonds out of the mouth of the Amazon River. It was absolutely catastrophic to me. We would be separated. He planned to be gone for two years on this great adventure, but we planned for it emotionally and every other way. We had a very melancholic Christmas in 1956 waiting for him to make this trip.

Did he actually go on this expedition?
Yes, he left in January. He and his friends got down to Mexico as far as Guaymas.

How were they traveling?
One of them had a beat-up old car.

They were going to drive down to the Amazon?
(Laughter) Oh yes. Ray knew he wanted to be a writer. He wanted to travel, to see the world, have adventure. At the same time he wanted me, and he tried to juggle these things forevermore, really. All the early things were definitely there. I unearthed some letters from high school days just last week

and it's amazing how all the Carver themes were in these letters written when he was seventeen years old.

How did the expedition work out?

Well, the boys had a falling out. One of them turned out to be an alcoholic, even at that age, and cantankerous. The two other boys were closer to each other than to Ray. There was some kind of fight. It had to do with *(laughs)* a crawdad or some horrible creature they had caught in the water down there and brought back to camp. As I recall, Ray caught this thing and was proud of it, and the drunk ridiculed it, and to make a long story short, they had a fight over it. And so in a matter of three weeks after he left, Ray arrived back in Redding, California, which was close enough to his parents so they could come and get him. He was absolutely broke and hadn't had a thing to eat for about three days. His dad laughed about how Ray ate two breakfasts when he got him. That was the end of that adventure, and of course I was very glad that he was back. He came up to Yakima and worked there that spring until I graduated in June. He came to the formal dances at the school and brought his friends down. His friends went with my friends and we had a lovely spring.

What was the name of that school?

St. Paul's School for Girls, an Episcopalian school in Walla Walla.

Then you married shortly after you graduated?

Four days after I graduated. Ray planned the whole wedding with my family. He bought the rings and worked hard on it. He had just turned nineteen, but he was kind of ageless. He could go hunting or fishing with his father's friends, who were well up into their forties or older, and he'd be treated as if he were one of them.

Did you and Ray have any plans?

Well, all the time I was at the girls' school I was very idealistic and studious. I saw my role in life to be a scholar. I knew I wouldn't be happy unless we got a very good higher education. Nobody in Ray's family had ever gone to college, so there was no tradition for it. He hoped he could just read a lot, which he always did, and that would prepare him adequately to be a writer. He had an extraordinary vocabulary, just like my mother. I could ask Ray the meaning of any word, and he'd know exactly what it meant and how to spell it, but he didn't particularly like school. He wasn't a natural student the way I was. However, the biggest plan in our lives was for Ray to become a first-rate, world-class writer.

But eventually he did go to college?

Yes, but because it was in the late fifties, and he was the male, and I was the female, it was the logical thing along sexist lines in those days that he would be the one to go. I went along with that, because I knew I would eventually go too, because I was so motivated. But it was important that he get started in school as soon as possible, and he did.

What school did he go to?

He started in the fall of '57 at Yakima Community College and attended for a year before we moved to California.

What prompted the move to California?

My mother and younger sister had gone down to California on a trip, and my sister was gung-ho to move there. She had some friends there, and she was a great beauty and brain and full of life and wanted to be where the action was, which she thought was in California, not in Washington. My mother, who was a teacher, got a job down there in the Bay Area, but she also bought a house that appealed to her in Paradise, California, near Chico. She thought that Ray and I and the baby could move down and live in that house, because she didn't want to leave me behind in Washington. She also persuaded us to move down because there was a four-year college in Chico that Ray could go to.

What about your education?

As far as my going to college, although I was the one with the high grades and the law school scholarship, when I mentioned going to junior college in Yakima and wanted to go desperately – my sister offered to take care of our baby girl, who had been born in December – Ray said, "What are you going to do with the baby – put her in a suitcase?" That so inhibited me that I hung back and didn't go and decided to become a good mother and all that.

Was Ray eager for college then?

Well, I had pointed out to him all along that as a writer he would benefit from a good education. He needed to read good writers, to know about them, and history, and art –

How long was he at Chico?

He went there from 1958 to 1960. I might say at this point that when I went to private school I had to read twenty books over the summer, and when I had these lists of books, and Ray would accompany me to the library where I'd check out Tolstoy, Flaubert, and Chekhov, for example – well, Ray had never heard of these writers before. I read all these books and told him what they were about, showed him their styles and so forth. He'd look at them and realize there was more to read than Thomas Costain and Edgar Rice Burroughs.

What happened after the two years at Chico?

We moved over to Humboldt, where he went to the state university, and after a year I started there too. Actually, I don't think this is too well known, but for the first thirteen years of our marriage, one or the other or both of us were in college, without any money pursuing an education. Thirteen years . . .

Why do you suppose he didn't write about the academic life in his stories?

It wasn't his primary interest in life, though he did enjoy the many friends we had from school, and he enjoyed studying drama, history, and some of the literature he encountered in good classes. However, Ray was always rather eccentric – always his own person. He never, in those days, jumped through hoops to please anyone or to placate the system. For example, one time he signed up for one more course than he wanted to take, merely to have enough units on paper to qualify for a federal loan. He never attended the class and took an F in it, which brought his grade point down, but none of this bothered him, whereas if I took a course, I'd have to get an A in it.

Can you tell us the name of the first story he wrote and when he completed it?

All the time I was at St. Paul's, long before he met John Gardner or anyone else, Ray was taking a course from the Palmer Institute of Writing, which his father working at the mill paid for and was proud his son was taking.

Was this a home study course?

Yes, and Ray would religiously do those assignments. He'd feel very guilty if he didn't. Later on and always, if he weren't writing for any reason, he'd feel guilty just like in high school. He used to send me assignments all the time when I was at St. Paul's. Maybe it was a character sketch, like a heavy woman baking bread, and you could smell the bread. Or else maybe it was to describe a scene –

Aside from these correspondence school assignments, which would you call Ray's first story?

Well, he had written some science fiction stories before we moved to Chico, but when he got into John Gardner's writing class down there he stopped being interested in writing about little green monsters and the like. He began the he/she stories in a contemporary literary mode.

Can you recall a story he wrote at Chico?

Yes, he wrote "Furious Seasons," and it created a tremendous stir among his classmates and the faculty at Chico.

Was this the story he later included in his collection of the same name? When did he write it?

Yes. This was in 1959, because I remember the green house we lived in and how old the babies were then.

Was this while he was in John Gardner's class?

Yes.

What did Gardner think of the story?

Oh, I know he thought it was outrageously good and taught the hell out of it in Ray's class – I went to listen. He also included the story in the college literary magazine he and another faculty member, Lennis Dunlap, were editing at the time. But Gardner was very cool and sophisticated. He wasn't one to lose control of a relationship or be too carried away about any one student's work. His students were always challenged to outdo their last effort. But it was very obvious, reading between the lines, so to speak, that both Gardner and Dunlap knew they were encountering someone very special in Ray.

Which was the first story actually accepted by a publisher?

Ray's first story accepted was "Pastoral" by *Western Humanities Review*. He received two copies for payment. This was in 1962, when we were living in Humboldt. As a matter of fact, I still have the letter of acceptance. On the very same day *Target*, a magazine in Arizona, accepted Ray's poem "Brass Ring," his first poetry acceptance.

We were on top of the world. It seemed that if you did the right things, the right things would happen. It was incredibly encouraging. We were ecstatic and partied for three days. We interrupted our friends' dinner, the poets David and Charlene Palmer, to celebrate our great news, our great joy. They dropped everything and we called other friends, who called other friends. We called Dick and Bonnie Day and brought them into the celebration. The Days, Palmers, and Carvers were wonderful friends despite the fact that they were ten years older than we. They taught us, they helped us, and they loved us. Dick Day was Ray's writing professor at the time, and Dave Palmer was a master librarian at Humboldt and a published poet. His wife, Charlene, was a poet and a very fine painter as well. They were all dear, dear friends who rejoiced in every success Ray or we had.

Why had you moved to Humboldt from Chico?

Because there was work for Ray in the lumber industry. There was nothing in Chico except working in the college library for a dollar an hour.

How did things work out in Humboldt?

Ray graduated from Humboldt in 1963. The first year we were there I worked for the phone company, where I felt left out of school life and lonely in general. I had transferred over to Humboldt from the Chico office, and altogether I had been working at the phone company since I was eighteen. I'd started when my second baby, my son, Vance, was eight months old. I'd get a paycheck every two weeks and within half an hour the money would be gone. By the time I paid the babysitter and all the bills, there was nothing left, and then I'd work another two weeks being dead broke all the time. I didn't enjoy the work, though out of pride I excelled at it, and I didn't relate to the crass type of people I worked with. That was a bad year for me. I worked days, and Ray went to school days and worked in a mill at night, so it was a grim year for him too, except for a good writing class he was taking and for some friends he met at school.

Then one morning at ten o'clock when I was on coffee break, I was twenty-one years old, something snapped in me, and I left the building in a hurry saying I was ill and took myself over to Humboldt. By five o'clock I had been admitted to school – I had the registrar call long distance to St. Paul's for my SAT scores. He got me a loan for tuition and lined me up for subsequent scholarships, which I received every semester for two years. When Ray came home that night and I told him I was going to go to school too – that I'd found a house near the college, a nursery school for the kids nearby, and a part-time job, all in one day – he was just blown away *(laughs)*.

That's marvelous. How did it turn out?

From then on in, things were really pretty good for us there. Ray quit the mill and worked at the college library, and together we had lots of friends. For the next two years we both went to school. Ray graduated in midyear '63 and went down to Berkeley and got a job at the University of California in the biology library. I finished school in June and moved to Berkeley with the children. In the meantime, Professor Dick Day, a writer and a very close personal friend of ours, was working to get Ray a grant at the University of Iowa at the Writers' Workshop. And that summer the grant came through. Ray got a thousand dollars, and by August '63 we were off to Iowa City. We piled everything into our '53 Chevy, Old Faithful we called it, with a rack on the top that carried all our belongings, and the four of us were on our way.

What was it like for you when you arrived in Iowa?

Well, first we stayed at a trailer park, but then our application for student housing was approved. I had been great through all the moves and transitions that we had gone through up until then, but I did just sit down on the bed and cry when I saw the Quonset hut, a World War II relic that served as University of Iowa married student housing. There were cement floors, open cupboards in the kitchen, the hot water tank was in the middle of the living room floor. The children's room was like a cell with two little bunks and a tiny window. It was quite depressing. The weather was cold and I just sat there crying for a while. Actually I turned that place into one of the most charming homes we ever had. I was really challenged by it. I had to get down and paint the cement floors and go out to buy a carpet from the Salvation Army, made curtains for the open cupboards, and turn the place into something we could tolerate. And as always, we had hard times through those early years as students, whether we were in Berkeley, or Iowa, or Humboldt, or wherever.

You were living the Carver story.

Oh, but we also had a tremendous amount of fun. We were popular people, we had lots of friends, and we entertained a lot. We were young, and we loved good times. And when we didn't have friends over, Ray and I had our own party every single night of our lives. At the end of the day, when we completed our jobs and work at school and finished with the children, we'd get together for a cup of coffee, talk over the day, and laugh. Ray was a very funny man, and we were funny together. Year in and year out we were crazy in love with each other.

We had our first turkey that we prepared ourselves in Iowa. We not only put on a holiday dinner for our children but for half the workshop as well. I worked at the University Athletic Club, a country club, as a waitress to bring in the bulk of our living. I put the turkey in the oven, then I rushed off to work, and Ray watched the dinner and the children. When I got off work, we had a feast, a party, with our kids and our friends.

How did things break for you after that?

After that, my father died in January, and I had to go back to the West Coast with the children for a month. Losing my dad was a devastating blow to me. When I got back to Iowa, I had to go right back to work and try to get caught up financially. I felt sad and very pressured. That spring, Ray went through a bout of depression himself, which he frequently did because of our financial struggle. We'd studied existentialism, and angst and melancholy went with the trade in those days, and Ray was good at it. However, he told me long after we were married that from an early age, before I had ever met him, as a teenager he'd considered suicide several times.

Had Ray started his heavy drinking by then?

No, he would drink at a time of crisis or something, and we would drink socially on some weekends, but alcohol definitely wasn't a major problem then.

How was his writing going at the time?

Ray wrote well in Iowa – for example "Sixty Acres," "The Student's Wife," "Will You Please Be Quiet, Please?" That spring, after we had had such a desperate time financially and all that, I checked around and found out that Ray had more publications than anybody else in the workshop. But he was very quiet, and very shy, and sat in the back of the room, and didn't impose himself on anybody, and the powers that be simply didn't know he was there. They'd champion other writers who weren't anywhere near as good as Ray. I don't want to name names, but the fact of the matter is nobody has ever heard of them again with the exception of Joy Williams. That's exactly what I went down and told Paul Engle when I found out they were deciding on grants for the following year. They were reading manuscripts for the grants that weekend, and Ray hadn't been invited to participate. I was a bit of a firebrand in those days, especially when it came to my family. I was going to make sure we survived. I was so angry. Ray had worked so hard at his writing and was so good, head and shoulders above everyone else, yet nobody knew he was even there.

He received no attention whatsoever, and we were starving practically.

What did you do?

Well, one morning I got my hair done *(laughs)* and put on my best dress. I didn't tell Ray, but I gathered all his published stories, and his manuscript in progress, which was "Will You Please Be Quiet, Please?" and I went down to the Writers' Workshop. I went down at 8 A.M. to Paul Engle's office and asked to see him. He wasn't there, and I said, that's fine, I'll wait. I waited all day. The secretary started looking at me, and so did all the writers and the faculty one by one, as they came in and heard the story *(laughs)*. Ray loved this story. A few years ago they asked him to attend an event at the University of Iowa honoring Paul Engle, and Ray wrote me how well he remembered this incident and how pleased he was I'd done what I had. Anyway, I just sat there all day with Ray's stuff and nothing to eat, and finally around four in the afternoon Paul Engle showed up. He asked me into his office, but he picked up his mail at the same time. He asked me what was on my mind, but when I started to tell him, he kept reading his mail. So I stopped talking, and after two minutes he noticed that, but I told him it was OK, why don't you just finish reading your mail. He realized of course that he'd been rude and pushed the mail aside and began listening to me. I asked him if he remembered what happened when Tennessee Williams came to Iowa. Everybody there knew how Williams had written *The Glass Menagerie* and the teachers there had rejected it, not given him his degree, and had virtually ridden him out of town on a rail. Engle perked up his ears. He was half insulted and half interested. I told him he had another situation almost exactly like that with my husband. Nobody knows he's here, nobody knows he exists, and nobody even reads his manuscripts. I told him Ray had more published stories and poems than any other student there, and he was a far better writer than many of the faculty members. I showed Engle all the publications, and the work in progress, and he agreed to give it to a faculty member to read over the weekend. The upshot of it was that John Clellan Holmes went wild over it after reading the manuscripts. He came back on Monday raving about Ray's work and passed it around to other powers that were.

How did Ray react to all this?

Talk about Ray's drinking – well, when Ray came back to the house *(laughs)*, he noticed his manuscripts were gone. Tampering with Ray's work was just anathema. It was his baby. I wasn't to touch works in progress, the kids weren't to touch them. His career, his writing, he and I put it on such a pedestal, we'd sacrifice anything for that, first, last, and always. Anyway, he noticed his things were gone, and when I fessed up what I had done, he stayed drunk all weekend *(laughs)*. He was actually pleased.

What was the result of your effort?

After the faculty read the stories, they offered him a stipend for the following year.

That must have been gratifying. Did it make life easier?

No, we went back to California in June.

Why?

As I said, my father had died. My father was the first hero in my life, and Ray was my next. My father's death was hard on me, and I was homesick for the coast. However, I didn't want to leave, because I wanted Ray to get his master's from Iowa, but Ray himself wanted to go back.

He wanted to quit?

Yes, Ray felt he wanted to move on at the time. The grass must be greener elsewhere and so on. Other people were packing up because it was time to go, and Ray got itchy feet too. Ray even quit the English Department at Berkeley when he was teaching there. He had a job teaching creative writing and he turned down a second year. We heard he was only the second person in history to quit the English Department at Berkeley.

When did he have that job at Berkeley?

1972, '73, when Lenny Michaels recommended him for the job. I'm just making the point that Ray always did what he wanted to do. If he wanted to leave Iowa before he got his degree there, and his emotional urge was such that he wanted to do it, he would do it. He was never compromised by awards or thoughts of future gain. He wasn't on any treadmill. He thought for himself.

After Iowa, did you go back to
Washington or California?

California. When we came back, we went to Sacramento, where Ray's parents lived. We had a hard time then. Ray had a hard time finding work. He had his B.A. from Humboldt, and a year at Iowa. He had been in school since 1957 and it was now 1964, but nobody was impressed with his credentials. He tried all kinds of little jobs. One job was as desk clerk in a hotel. *(Laughs)* Before he put in one shift, he had me deliver a letter to them telling them he wouldn't be coming. He worked as a stock boy at Weinstock's Department Store. There's this father of two children, a writer with all these publications, and his degree, and he's working as a stock boy. The final blow came when he was fired for stealing cookies, and of course he hadn't taken their cookies. Somebody else had, but they fired the whole crew. These were hard times for Ray. I was working. I always worked. I always had to.

Did Ray keep up with his writing?

Yes, he never stopped writing. That was always his main focus along with me and the family. He had a job as janitor at Mercy Hospital in Sacramento, and he was glad to get it. He held that job for two and a half years. First on the day shift, where he really had to work, mopping, housekeeping, and doing hospital beds. Then he got on the night shift, which was a gravy train, and he had his days free to write.

Do you remember which stories he wrote during
this time?

I guess I could just go down the table of contents of the collection *Will You Please Be Quiet, Please?* I edited every one of those stories before anybody did. Ray would encourage me to do what John Gardner did, take a pencil and strike out any words I thought didn't belong. I was perfectly free to edit a story or poem in any way. And without fail he would take fifty percent of my suggestions and ignore the other fifty percent. We'd sit down with a story, and I'd explain my corrections, and he'd agree or not. But it was always a joint effort to come out with the best.

Did you recognize yourself in these stories?
Oh, I saw myself in these stories, of course, but Ray was a fiction writer, and he took liberties, God knows.

Could you tell us something about Ray's work habits?
Whenever he could afford it, Ray would rent a room where he could be alone to do his writing. Even in 1961, when we had a big house in Arcata, which was the first time he rented space away from home, he rented a room elsewhere to write in. He had one later in Sacramento, he had one later in Palo Alto, and in Cupertino. We sacrificed necessities and certainly luxuries so he could rent space where he could write. All those stories about him only having space to write in his car are all part of a projected poor me syndrome that adds to the drama of his success.

When we were in Sacramento, we had two salaries. He had his job in the hospital, and I was office manager at Parents Magazine Cultural Institute. My immediate supervisor there was Werner Erhard, who later founded est. Werner and I were good friends and would fly around to major cities to give addresses at various hotels. I had this job that made lots of money, and Ray was working at the hospital at that time. Werner was manager of the San Francisco office, and I was manager of the Sacramento office. I had never made so much money in my life. I'd had two years of college by then, and because of the poverty and Ray's and my situation, I had to drop out of Sacramento State even though I was making straight A's and almost through with the semester, then the cookie thing came up and there was no money. I went around with tears running down my cheeks when I checked out of all my classes, and I went to work as a barmaid to pay everybody. The lights were turned off at our house at one time, and then when we couldn't pay the rent, I took the children and went to my mother's in Paradise, California, and Ray had to go live with his parents. That was a real low point in the fall of '64 when we came back from Iowa. Then in January '65 I got the job at Parents and got out of the bar where I'd worked as a cocktail waitress, the first time I'd ever done that. At Parents I just rose in the ranks. There was an opportunity to make money, dress well, use my intelligence, and I went for it. Before long I was wearing hundred-dollar dresses from Magnin's, and I had a maroon Pontiac convertible. We all started living the high life, you know. I knew in my heart that I would go back to college, that I really was a scholar, but it was such a relief for a while not to have this money worry. I felt like a thousand-pound weight had been lifted off my head.

That sounds like a relief all right. What stopped it?
Well, Ray. *(Laughs)* Ray did. He got jealous of my job and the power and attention I had there. Werner had told me to define the job I'd like to do. Of course Werner and I were working with the materials that produced the foundation of the human growth movement in California – in the world. We were right in there pioneering that, reading all the books – *Psychocybernetics, As a Man Thinketh, The Games People Play*, and all those.

You say Ray became jealous?
Well, there were these two handsome, brilliant men, Werner Erhard and Raymond Carver, in my life. One was my boss, and we'd go out to dinner and discuss business. I'd drive in my convertible that was faster than the wind, which I had thanks to my job, dressed in fancy clothes. In the meantime Ray had this janitor job at the hospital, which was OK for him for a while as it meant security, and it gave him time to get a lot of writing done, but certainly no prestige associated with what he was doing. Werner thought it was a great idea when I defined my job as flying around to all the cities that had branches of this company and take employees out to cultural events to refresh them and give them another frame of reference. At that point Ray got a job as editor at SRA in Palo Alto, the first white-collar job he ever had. He then gave me an ultimatum – your marriage or your job. Werner and I didn't have a romance. It was just a work association, no hanky panky what-

soever, but Ray decided to become head of the family with a vengeance just at that time.

I remember looking in the mirror and facing this enormous dilemma. I had to choose between a job I just loved, or the man I loved. As it happened so many times when I had wonderful career opportunities, I had to turn them down because Ray and his career came first.

So after the ultimatum . . .

It was tough, because I was used to running an office, making good money, and now all of a sudden – nothing. So I went back to college and eventually graduated from San Jose State, where I got my teaching credentials. I missed all the excitement of the job, but the thing I could always do was get A's in school in everything.

So, to create some new excitement in my life, in the first semester at San Jose, this is spring '68 by now, I applied for a scholarship in the California State College Study Abroad program. They reviewed our application carefully, and it was just an incredible one, because Ray was a writer with all these publications to his credit, and yet we had these two children, so it would take a lot more money for a family to go abroad for a year than just a single student. Ours was a special and complex situation, so they made an exception, and we were accepted as a family. We were finally going to get to travel, which is what we had wanted for years and years to do.

Well, we were incredibly excited, high as kites. I was such a good student that we had our choice to go anywhere – Uppsala, Sweden; or Florence, Italy; or Tel Aviv, Israel. Now as I view my grand life design, I see Israel was the absolutely perfect place for me given my later interest in spiritual realities. To have had the opportunity at that age to go to the Holy Land was astounding planning on a higher plane when I think of how my life has gone since that time. We went there because *(laughs)* we were offered an extra five hundred dollars. Later Ray regretted we hadn't gone to Florence, because of his interest in the Renaissance and the art in that lovely city.

What was it like for Ray in Israel?

We only stayed four months. We were supposed to stay a whole year. Ray and my daughter both became very disgruntled. My son and I loved it. Ray had been publishing a lot of stories and poems just before we left. He was very eager to travel, but when we got over there, he'd say, I don't know what I'm doing in Asia. We had an apartment which was small by our standards, only two bedrooms, but actually we had the apartment of the conductor of the Israel Philharmonic. By Israeli standards, we had a very special place with paintings and wonderful art objects in the apartment. But Ray would sit out on the balcony and clutch his copy of *Life on the Mississippi (laughs)* and sit there muttering America First, America First, which was pretty wild because this was 1968, and Robert Kennedy, whom I had voted for, had been shot, and Martin Luther King had been shot, and all that was going on on the college campuses, the rallies and so forth. But for us, the trip to Israel made us appreciate our country, right or wrong.

Given that, did you stay much longer in Israel?

Well, we had been promised a villa on the Mediterranean, but they decided to use that villa for twelve students. Ray resented that we didn't have the villa, and the children weren't in English-speaking schools as promised. The children went to school in the old Arab city of Jaffa, and it took about an hour and a half to get there with three bus transfers. One day a bomb went off in a wastebasket in the bus depot, killing six people just fifteen minutes after our children were there. Ray was upset. He said, This may be the high time of your life, studying at the university, learning Hebrew, and listening to Golda Meir speak, and dancing Jewish folk dances, but I'm going to take my children and go home. There again I was faced with another ultimatum. Except he had lined up a cruise from Haifa to Venice, first class for the regular cruise fare by telling them he was a writer and would write an article about them. He told me we would stop in Athens and all the Greek islands, and we'd send the kids home first and travel through Europe. And we did do all that.

So after you returned home . . . ?

Ray wound up after awhile teaching at Iowa. He had already taught at Berkeley and Santa Cruz, and also received the Wallace Stegner fellowship at Stanford. His friends not only called him Running Dog at that point, but also called him Feather in the Wind. He kept his job teaching in Santa Cruz while teaching in Iowa and flew back and forth without either school knowing about it.

Now that's a no-no –

(Laughs) Well, Ray did all the no-no's. He did what he wanted. He was a renegade.

When did Ray first show signs of his alcoholism?

When his drinking pattern changed. We had always drunk socially, and occasionally we did get drunk. We didn't know alcoholism was a disease. We'd drink at a weekend party, but it was always a safe thing, because we'd look out for each other. As I said it was only on occasion, and when it happened we thought it was funny. We took care of each other, and no harm done. It was only when he taught the first year at the university that his drinking habits changed.

Was this at Iowa or Santa Cruz?

Santa Cruz. This was after we came back from Israel. I was teaching at Los Altos High School. The first year I taught, Ray had a whole year off where he could write, and he wrote many, many stories. He finished the bulk of *Will You Please Be Quiet, Please?*

What year was this?

That was in 1971. Ray was, to begin with, essentially a very shy person and introverted. Of course once he got to know people, and with friends he was different. *Will You Please Be Quiet, Please?* wasn't published until 1976, and for five years Ray didn't draw a sober breath. He left his job at University of California, Santa Barbara, a semester early due to his health, and after that he wasn't able to work until 1978.

How did you get by?

I had to support everybody. Get up at six in the morning.

We had to sell our house – *(She stops to draw a few deep breaths. We take a break.)*

> *Let's try it this way. Could you tell us more about when Ray started drinking heavily, and perhaps what you consider may have been the cause?*

As I said, his drinking habits changed when he started to teach. He was very shy. He had gone back to Iowa, before he taught at Santa Cruz, in the summer of '67 to study to be a librarian, because he liked libraries. He liked quiet little cubicles where he could work with books and magazines. Dick Day and some of his other friends wrote letters of recommendation, and he was accepted to get his master's degree in library science. But shortly after he started in that program, his father died, and Ray had to come back to California to bury his father, and so he got away from that. Then when he began to teach, it was a whole different thing. To be up in front of a class or group of people was terrifying for him. It was against his nature, though he became very good at it.

I had cooked up this teaching job for him through friends who knew James B. Hall, the provost of the program called College V at Santa Cruz based on the Oxford system of individual colleges. Ray was flattered to get the job, but he would drink the moment he got out of class. He'd have several drinks, and his whole drinking pattern changed. He drank around his job, although he did an excellent job there. He put out a college magazine and worked with a group of good young writers.

> *How long did that last?*

Well, the following summer in 1972 Ray took a trip to Montana. He knew Bill Kittredge by then, and on this trip he made contact with a group of writers in Montana who did a lot of drinking. We always used to joke about how when Ray would go up there to visit, he was amazed to see that these men got up and showered and shaved and put on fresh starched shirts and dressed up at eight in the morning as if they were going off to work, when what they were doing was going off to drink.

Didn't you accompany him on these trips?

Yes, I went up there with him once, but he'd go without me, as I had my teaching job by then.

Did you look upon them as a drinking crowd?

Yes, and people who were divorced, and into their second and third wives and so forth. The slogan was another wife, another life. Remember, this was the seventies. There was a lot of disillusionment, the me-first generation. Women's lib came into flower, women were wanting divorces. Ray and I seemed like the last holdouts. We were ridiculed by all sorts of people, because we were still together, high school sweethearts. The other writers would say, "This reminds me of my first marriage." These were people now on their third or fourth, and they were great authorities with a couple of novels published. I'm not going to name names, but they were taking scenes from our life and putting them into their novels, making a satire of our lives. They'd say, "Get a divorce and grow." They were into a much wilder life-style than we'd ever had. And hanging out with this crowd, Ray became hopelessly addicted to alcohol.

Wasn't Ray writing from his experience about men having a problem holding on to their liquor, their marriages, their jobs?

People get into such generalities. Ray was a fiction writer. His work is not strictly autobiographical. Many incidents happened that were kernels of stories, but he had the dramatic sense to make them into a story that people would sit up and notice. The fact is that all happy families are alike, as Tolstoy observed, but unhappy families are unhappy in a unique way. Ray fastened on what was unhappy and unique in a situation and was able to create a dramatic story rather than a bland tale with no tension. A lot of times, as I've said, he'd take a kernel of something that really happened and convert it into a fine story.

Could you give us an example?

Well, take "Will You Please Be Quiet, Please?" That came out in 1967, just before we went to Israel, and was chosen for the *Martha Foley Collection of Best American Short Stories* of that year. I have an original copy upstairs in my bedroom. When that story came out, people were outraged or titillated to know just what the real situation had been. We'd go to parties and everybody was looking at me, and some would ask me, but I simply said that I'll never tell. It was important for Ray's career and his stories for me not to tell. It was rude of them to ask if it really happened or not. We knew that stories are stories.

Or take the story "Are These Actual Miles?" I actually went out and sold my Pontiac convertible. It was my car, and I sold it, but how I sold it was nobody's business. Ray's story wasn't life. It was his story from an incident in our lives that captured his imagination, and Ray wrote it.

I know Ray created art out of life, but I always thought that particular story was especially close to his experience. The narrator is drinking heavily –

You know, Ray's father was an alcoholic, his grandfather was an alcoholic. They both died indirectly of alcoholism and nobody ever said alcoholism. It wasn't recognized as a disease, as people look upon it today. Ray was around enough drinkers and mill workers to know about people who drink too much. It was not us in 1967 when he wrote a story. We did do some recreational drinking in Sacramento, but it wasn't the wild out-of-control drinking of the seventies after he started teaching at Santa Cruz. There was never a serious problem with alcohol before.

And then when it became a problem?

When it became a problem, he couldn't write. No stories were written when he was desperately drunk. He wrote those stories about people drinking when he was sober. It's how it was.

As I sit here listening to you, I cannot help thinking of the woman narrating Ray's story "Chef's House" –

Yes, I lived with Ray in Chef's house, but what happened wasn't exactly like the story. There are resemblances of course. He was happy I was still wearing my wedding ring, for example. What really happened in Chef's house was that at Christmas time he saw John Cheever on "The Dick Cavett Show." He had been friends with and drunk with Cheever back in Iowa, and here was his friend Little John and Dick Cavett talking about being a writer in New York. Ray made the decision to go east and be a writer there and did so in January, when he went back east to Goddard College. He uprooted the Chef's house to follow the route of John Cheever, whom he saw on a TV show. He had been sober since June of 1977, and by December he was ready to go. That's what happened at Chef's house. Also Ray was writing well again in "Chef's House." He wrote "Why Don't You Dance?" and "Viewfinder" there, for example. He felt well by Christmas.

Not exactly the same as the story, was it?
No, Chef didn't take his house back to give to his daughter, for example.

Bankruptcy appears in many of Ray's stories and poems. Was that close to your experience?
Well, we did get into debt in Sacramento. It was a debt we had been paying, and I expected to continue making the payments. Ray got tired of that and suggested bankruptcy. We had a major disagreement about that. I was adamantly opposed to it, adamantly, adamantly, adamantly opposed to it.

Ray made that clear enough in those stories and poems. Why were you so opposed?
It wasn't my upbringing. My family upbringing was different. My family were teachers and landowners. My mother was a teacher.

Chris Carver

I paid my rent from my job working in an all-girl gas station and bought my first car before I was sixteen. My mom was broken-hearted that I wasn't living at home, but I wouldn't go back. Things were

Chris Carver is ready with the coffee and a box of doughnuts. The interview takes place on a cool gray Saturday morning in her modest tract house in Ferndale, Washington. A Carver house. She shows me her keepsakes, her father's books and letters. She is apprehensive about the interview. When she first speaks of her father, it approaches reverence. Her eyes moisten. She reads aloud a few Carver poems to me. We chat about the last time we met at a small shopping mall outside Vancouver, where she, Maryann, and I had gone to see *Short Cuts*, the movie based on some of Carver's stories. I recalled that while we waited in line, Maryann, in the course of striking up a conversation with a bright young couple, revealed that she was the former wife of Raymond Carver. Maryann was unfazed as the couple nodded politely at this puzzling information. It was obvious they had never heard of Raymond Carver. Chris laughs as she says that her dad would have loved that story. We each have a doughnut in hand as we start the interview.

What are your early memories of your father?
This would be when I came home from kindergarten in Iowa. I remember my dad taking care of me and being around home much of the time. In fact, he took care of my brother, Vance, and me a lot. Until we had a washer and dryer of our own, I can remember my dad loading up sheets full of laundry and taking them down to the laundromat. I recall him mopping our kitchen floors and sitting down with Vance and me and us eating peanut butter toast or cheese and crackers. If Vance and I fought over something, Dad would have us draw straws or he'd have us flip a coin. He'd joke that he'd give us a knuckle sandwich or knuckle rub if we didn't behave.

I remember coming home from school to find a U-Haul trailer at our house and finding out we were moving to California.

Was that the move to Sacramento?
Yes. I remember after we settled in there Mom and Dad

would load us all into the car to go to Reno for a day or two. They'd drop us off at a movie theater for all-day Disney movies while they'd go gambling, then they'd pick us up and we'd go to a casino for dinner and Vance and I would have Shirley Temples and Roy Rogers.

What else can you recall about that time in Sacramento?

Well, we were in one house for a full year, and I believe my dad was working as a janitor in a hospital. At that time, we had this big white fluffy dog named Mitzi. My dad didn't like the hassle of the dog because she did chew up the furniture and clothes, and there was an ongoing concern with fleas, heats, and batches of puppies. Dad couldn't handle all this. In fact, it's a true story that he did take the dog and dumped her somewhere. Then he did bring Mitzi back, as my brother and I were heartsick over missing her. Vance and I would cry for her all night until we saw Dad pull into the driveway one night with Mitzi in the back seat.

So there we have his story, "Jerry and Molly and Sam" –

Yes, he originally called it "The Dog Story." Then we moved to another house next to a restaurant called Paisano's. I remember this very well because I went to two grades from that house. You see, I associate each of Dad's stories with where we were living at the time. The house in Sacramento which would have been '64 or '65 – that's where "The Dog Story" came from, and the story "The Bath" (later called "A Small Good Thing") was based on the time I was hit by a car while riding my bicycle. I had a bleeding gash in my calf, but the mother and son who hit me stopped, looked, and then drove on. Dad couldn't get over that people could be like that. We went over that many times. Even the story "Fever," which was published many years later, came from that house. My mom was away a lot then working for Parents Institute, and my dad was home with us kids all that time. In the story the father hires a housekeeper as he worries about his son getting sick while trying to cope with the absence of his wife. We actually did have this housekeeper who cooked up fried potatoes and prepared hot meals for us every night. My dad literally cried when she had to leave us. Just like in the story.

Did he write "Will You Please Be Quiet, Please?" around this time?

That story I believe originated in the house we lived in for a year before this one. I read that story a couple of times as a kid and told my dad I didn't understand the ending. He made a point to tell me that fiction didn't need to be factual, and that I would understand his themes someday. But let me go back to the Sacramento house. The story "What Is It?" (later called "Are These Actual Miles?") came from there too. My mom and dad had bought this beautiful red Pontiac convertible. My mom would put the top down and take me with her sometimes when she had meetings with her co-workers. But when she was away much of the time working, my dad would pack up Vance and me and take us to the Sacramento River for swimming and fishing. Or he'd take us to a drive-in movie. Our whole family liked movies.

Can you recall anything more of life in Sacramento?

My parents got a job managing apartments in exchange for their rent. I thought it was heaven because it had a swimming pool. "The Bridle" comes from those apartments. My parents became good friends with the Holletts, who were horse people from Minnesota and living upstairs in the apartments. Every night our families partied out by the pool. Bill Holletts on a dare jumped one night from the apartment right into the pool. We were all amazed, especially my dad, who laughed until he cried.

Right out of "The Bridle."

Yes, the pool incident was bizarre. I know that's where Dad got the idea for the material. There are a lot of stories that I can completely relate with where he got the idea for the story because I was there. I'm not saying that he – after all any artist will bring experience to their material, but when completed, it would not be art if not for the manipulation before the final product. And also I must say that my dad was a sensitive and intuitive man who would take in moments and events and internalize them to such a degree that he was able to see the humor and tragedy of these events, and his gift compelled him to write, write, write.

Where did the Carver family go after Sacramento?

Dad got a job with the publishing firm SRA in Palo Alto. We lived for a year in a lovely home that was rented from a Stanford professor on sabbatical. We all had our own bedroom and the house had two bathrooms. Dad went to work wearing a suit every day, his first white-collar job actually. He had a study where he did his writing and it was off-limits to Vance and me. Once we got into his trunk full of manuscripts and things he had going at the time and we got a whipping for it. I know he had been writing up a storm there – stories and some of the poems that were later published in *Winter Insomnia*. He'd be writing all the time up there in his study and going to his job every day in a suit. In his spare time we'd go to the horse races at Bay Meadows and to the San Francisco Giants games. We also still went to a lot of movies.

How long did you stay in Palo Alto?

This lasted barely a year, because then my mother received a scholarship to go abroad, which was a major decision for my parents, but after finding out there were English-speaking schools for Vance and me, they decided to go. So we all packed up and went to Israel.

How did your father take to Israel?

He thought the idea of living and studying abroad would be prestigious and adventuresome, but he became miserable there. The food for one thing and he didn't have anything going for him there. We had to travel from one market to the next with a net bag just to get basics for dinner. The whole process would take over half a day. Dad's stomach couldn't take the sight of separating milk in the fridge or chicken claws popping out of boiling water pans. Vance and I had to ride an hour and a half every day with a strange English family to get to a school in the old Arab city of Jaffa. As usual, my parents had many friends, but each person they knew had horrible Holocaust stories directly or of their families. We enjoyed the people from the university who took us to traditional dances, basketball games, and to the beach, but it was my mom's gig really. After four months my dad insisted we pack it up and go home, which turned out to be a good thing, as we ended up taking a cruise on a Greek liner through all the Greek islands, then we rented a car and drove from Italy to France and stayed in Paris for a while. Then they put my brother and me on an airplane and shipped us home to my Aunt Amy, while they had a little vacation in Paris alone together.

And when you all got back together, where did you live?

My Aunt Amy got us a house near her in Hollywood, California, where she'd been studying to be an actress for many years. My dad sold programs at the Cineramadome theater. A few months later my mother got into the university at San Jose, so we moved there. We were in student housing that was just like a little cracker box of a place. It was a hard place to live in – old military housing that they converted into student family housing right across the street from Spartan Stadium with its football games and rock concerts. This was in the late sixties and there were antiwar marches and demonstrations going on. It got so bad that at that time my dad rented a room somewhere where he could write. My brother made friends with a black family of boys. They were called the Brown brothers because their last name was Brown, but their mother had remarried and had the last name Green. Our family and theirs would go over to the stadium and have fantastic baseball games with my dad always as team captain. Everyone wanted to be on his team.

But as I said the housing situation was so poor, and we were all relieved when my mom graduated and got a job teaching English at the high school in Los Altos. We moved to a nice house nearby in Sunnyvale. Dad was writing, Mom was teaching, and Vance and I were making long-lasting friends. Then my dad got a job teaching at Santa Cruz, so my mom and dad decided to move there. They were not quite thirty and Santa Cruz was considered a hip place to be at the time. I was twelve then, just starting junior high. Mom was teaching at Los Altos, driving an hour and a half each way every day.

Would this this be about the time that drinking became a serious problem?

OK, I remember this as a high time in my family's life when we were in Santa Cruz, because they had a lot of friends celebrating literary achievements. Charles Bukowski partied at our house, for example, along with my parents' dear friends, the Houstons and Swangers, and as always my Aunt Amy. All the things that my parents had worked so hard for and dreamed about were beginning to come true for them. My dad's work was becoming recognized, he received a Stegner fellowship at Stanford and the Joseph Henry Jackson award naming him the best writer in California for the year. He had many friends and there was a lot of socializing. Then he lost his job at Santa Cruz and got more involved with the Missoula people, Chuck Kinder, Bill Kittredge, Jim Crumley, and Richard Hugo. There was even some talk of moving to Missoula for a teaching job, but after a lot of discussion my parents decided not to move again. That's when we bought the house in Cupertino, a home where we lived for nearly four years.

Cupertino is where I really remember the drinking. Shortly after we moved there, my dad took a trip by himself to Missoula to visit his writing buddies. While on a binge, he met another woman. When he returned, his drinking escalated and it began undermining every aspect of family and work structure he had, and my childhood as I had known it had changed and was gone forever. But at the time we didn't recognize the drinking as a serious problem. We didn't know much about alcoholism in those days. Nobody could say, There's a white elephant in your living room and it's the alcohol. You cannot blame anybody for what went on. It's part of the disease of alcoholism to put blame on everyone and everything, but my dad was an existentialist and he would be the first to say that you have to take responsibility for your actions. The compounding problems from the drinking took its toll on everyone. It's tragic how two people in love, with such great ideals and talent, became victims of this disease. The infidelity broke my mother's heart, which took her years to overcome, and my dad suffered horribly as well.

It was also frustrating for my dad because back then short stories weren't selling, and the success wasn't happening fast enough, and besides their whole crowd was drinking. Everybody was doing it. I remember seeing Dad drink in the daytime, and I had never seen him do that before.

Despite all that, at the time he was on the verge of breaking through with his collection of Will You Please Be Quiet, Please?

Yes, I'd come home from school and he'd be surrounded with sheets of paper, which were the galleys of *Will You Please Be Quiet, Please?* He'd explain this was what happens when you publish a book. He'd have me help him correct and organize the connecting pages, but he was also drinking screwdrivers. We spent a lot of time together.

How old were you at the time?

Fourteen, fifteen. His friends can attest that I was there at all the parties. Whether the parties were at our house, or the Kinders' or Ungers' in San Francisco, we would all pitch in making the big dinners. My mom and I would make up gigantic breakfasts. They taught me how to make big strong pots of coffee, and how to make their drinks, and I drank along with them. I had my own life, but they were a lot of fun and a hell of an interesting crowd to be around. It was between the parties my dad found it hard to cope, and so he drank daily. It was a wild time and very destructive to his writing and ability to teach. The whole family would get into horrible fights. We'd sit down to the dinner table and my dad would be drunk and he'd start egging my brother on. He'd have my brother in tears. One time he started badgering me, and I picked up a hot roller set and tossed it through the sliding glass door, glass shattering everywhere. Once, he wiped out my savings account from working. There were just scenes all the time. If my parents got into fights, sometimes my dad and I would sit at the table far into the night counseling and processing the events. The same would go for my mother and me.

I remember him having a terrible fight with my mom, and this is in a story he wrote later on. He was packing up a bag that didn't even latch, and it was an emotional scene. He was drunk and packing the bag and saying to us, "Well, I guess that's it. Your mother wants me to go, so I may as well move. I'll pack it all up and go." And Vance and I are standing there crying, "No, Dad, no. Please don't go." Then we all were crying and hugging each other. Dad did not go. It was like that scene in "Short Cuts" during the earthquake when the Jerry, Molly, and Sam family are holding on to each other.

Wasn't this also the time he was in Iowa?

Yes, he was gone there for six or seven months. Cheever was there with him. He flew back a couple of times to visit us. Mom and he didn't separate. They still stayed together, but when the Iowa stint was over, because of everything I'd seen I didn't accept him as an authority figure anymore. He'd order me around and I just wouldn't take it anymore. There were some horrible scenes when he was drunk where he'd batter me up. Once the police came and they wanted to handcuff me and take me away, but my Aunt Amy came to my rescue. There were so many family problems that were directly related to the drinking that I moved out of the house when I was fifteen.

Where did you go?

I moved in with my Aunt Amy, who had a place in Mountain View nearby. I paid my rent from my job working in an all-girl gas station and bought my first car before I was sixteen. My mom was broken-hearted that I wasn't living at home, but I wouldn't go back. Things were happening there that were directly related to the stories "Where Is Everyone?" and "Are These Actual Miles?" Actually I did go back when my aunt went to Iowa to get her M.F.A. degree. Then my dad was offered a job to teach in Santa Barbara. We packed everything in two cars and caravanned down to Santa Barbara. The drinking was so bad at that point that he couldn't hold down his job there. I had two phone calls in the space of two weeks where I had to go bail my parents out of jail at four in the morning. I remember this as the ultimate in humiliation for me and my parents. And once when we were in a restaurant, he was so drunk that he started calling me horrible names out loud. I left them at the restaurant, packed up my car, and started up to Mountain View, where my grandmother lived. I left a note begging them not to try to find me, to give me a break just like the poem "Next Year" in *Where Water Comes Together with Other Water*. Anyway, my car, an old Corvair, broke down in the middle of the night in King City only halfway to Mountain View. Here I was, a teenage girl in a place like that so late at night. A sheriff picked me up and took me to Juvenile Hall. They tried to locate my dad in Santa Barbara, but he was sitting around drunk, not answering the phone. Finally, King City police contacted the police in Santa Barbara, who sent a sheriff to the house to tell my dad where I was detained. My mother, who had been frantic, sent a bus ticket to Santa Barbara to me, which was the last place I wanted to be. I had just gone through all this to get away from their problems, give me a break, why would I want to go back?

Anyway, they came to pick me up in King City. I told them that I loved them, but I couldn't go through all this again. They didn't remember and were still hazy about what had gone on in the restaurant. I told them I would get a job and go to alternate school while I lived with Grandma in Mountain View. They let me do it and I worked so hard in school that I graduated a year ahead of my regular class.

Where did they go from there?

They went to San Francisco as they had rented out the house in Cupertino. They lived near the Kinders and the Ungers. None of us had a home anymore. I remember thinking that this whole family is so dysfunctional. I'd show up there and all the lights would be on blazing.

I moved into the apartment adjoining the Cupertino house, and from time to time my dad would come down from San Francisco, visit with me and some of his old buddies from Stanford. He'd pull out a pint of vodka and we'd sit around out in the backyard patio and talk about all sorts of things. Even in the worst of times, we never totally fell out. And it was about this time that my parents began their attempts to sober up with the help of their friends and AA.

Didn't your parents make an attempt to get back on

*track about then up in McKinleyville? The place Ray
wrote about in "Chef's House"?*

Yes, I was supposed to stay there with them because of
some trouble that I had gotten into, but I had a job in Sunnyvale, so I'd come up and visit them, check in, as often as I
could. My brother was staying with a teacher friend of my
mother's. It was a fragile time for all of us, a time to get over
some of the bad things that had gone on. Dad had quit drinking, and he'd go fishing every day, and my mom would go along
too. They had friends who'd take them mushroom picking, and
the two of them would make big salmon loaf dinners. When I
visited he'd let me drive his car. He was kind to me, good to
me. He was more like his old self. It was a lovely time, and we
all celebrated a beautiful Christmas together up there where
he gave me a copy of his book *Furious Seasons*, which had just
been published by his friend Noel Young at Capra Press. I
have it right here on this table. *(She reads the inscription.)*
For my darling daughter Chris, at Christmas 1977. With all
love. McKinleyville, California.

How long did they stay up there?

The next summer my parents joined my Aunt Amy and
Doug Unger in Iowa City, where the Ungers had house-sitting
prospects lined up. My dad had stopped drinking and had re-
gained enough confidence to start writing again and give readings. My mom threw a big fortieth birthday party for him with
printed napkins and all. The theme of the party went from
Running Dog to Dandy Dog.

That September my dad went to teach at El Paso and my
mother returned to Washington to care for my great-aunt,
who was ill. My parents did not rejoin after that.

How did you keep in touch with your father after that?

We'd keep in touch by phone. I felt sorry for him because
he told me he spent a lot of time alone at his place and wasn't
socializing yet with the new people in El Paso. He was still
sober, though, and then he got together with Tess Gallagher.
After that in all the time back and forth from Syracuse to Port
Angeles, he would call about twice a month and he'd also set
up a visit at the Holiday Inn in Bellingham, where he'd visit

me and my children usually twice a year until his death. On other occasions I'd visit him in Port Angeles. On one of those visits Dad told me to hold on to his letters as they might be of value to collectors someday. This was in 1983. I'd been keeping them, but after that I made a point to save every one of them.

What do you intend to do with these letters?

I'd like to publish them, because I believe they would be of great interest to scholars and all others interested in his work. Up to now there have been problems with some issues concerning copyright, but I understand the law has recently been changed as to who owns the copyright on personal letters, so I hope I may soon be allowed to get on with it. They are important letters expressing so many of his thoughts and ideas about his work, and right up to the end were full of support and unconditional love for me.

Douglas Unger

Carver was in very bad shape, but he did pull out of it somehow. He stopped drinking. Could you tell us how he managed to do that?

Well, Amy and I were a part of that, in for the long haul. Ray came to Iowa City that spring. There was continuing strife in his marriage. They were going to separate. Then they were going to stay together. They were going to split up again. A lot of it is shown in the stories in *What We Talk About When We Talk About Love* – the infidelity committed by the man that destroys trust, followed by all the guilt and heavy drinking. Stories such as "Gazebo" and "A Serious Talk" and "One More Thing." That was just about exactly what was going on in his life. That spring he came to Iowa City to give a reading. He was supposed to be on his way to Yaddo after that, but he got drunk the day of the reading and stayed so drunk he never made it out of town. He lived at our house in Iowa City for about two months. Then he went back to San Francisco to re-join Maryann and try to work through the problem.

How did that work out?

It was a rough time for everyone. We also moved to San Francisco that summer. That was when Ray began his rounds to attempt to quit drinking once and for all.

How long did that last?

He started to try to stop drinking from the summer of '76 through the fall and into '77. He had an apartment in San Francisco at first, and when he gave that up he would stay with us or with Chuck and Diane Kinder, who had a big apartment across the street. In between he would go back to live with Maryann. Amy and I rented our flat from the St. James Episcopal Church, where meetings of Alcoholics Anonymous were held. Maryann was the most influential in trying to help. She had sobered up first and was very serious about a twelve-step program. She was willing to do anything to save Ray. We all knew he was going to die if he didn't quit drinking. And he knew it too.

That was a grim time.

What happened next was he was affected by CNS seizures.

CNS seizures?

For a certain number of alcoholics, especially the heaviest drinkers, their nervous system has become so adjusted to having alcohol that when they stop drinking they go into seizures as though with epilepsy. These seizures are very dangerous. It's how brains are damaged during convulsions.

It's like "Where I'm Calling From."

Yes. Ray had hit the floor several times, like the character Tiny in that story. That's where the detail is from. Ray was the one who was on the floor with his heels clicking. He was then terrified to quit drinking, because it had happened in a hospital in San Francisco, and it had happened when he'd tried to quit on his own, so he kept on drinking. He and Maryann split up again. Ray began a relationship with another woman, who as in "Where I'm Calling From" was shortly after diagnosed as having cancer. That story is almost entirely taken from his life at that time.

But he did eventually stop?

As I said, he made so many attempts over that year and a half to stop drinking. Many of us were trying to help him. Once I accompanied Chuck Kinder and Ray to a summer home up in Tiburon, loaned to us for that purpose. Chuck and Ray were going to try to stop drinking together. But they weren't there four hours before they discovered a fully stocked liquor cabinet, and the whole thing turned into a kind of drinking contest between them.

Before that, Ray had rented a small apartment on Castro Street in San Francisco. Just like in "Careful," which describes that apartment exactly, Ray had somehow convinced himself that if he only drank champagne, he'd be able to taper off and quit. He'd go out in the morning and buy bottles of the cheapest André, but this wasn't working and he knew it. At that point everyone had given up hope. We all thought he would keep on drinking until it killed him. And he thought so too.

How did he come out of that?
What made him turn around?

As with so many important events in his life, it was Maryann. She had heard of a place called Duffy's, an alcoholic rehabilitation center in Myrtledale, California. She was selling the house in Cupertino and had scraped together the money for a rehab center for Ray. This place, Duffy's, is the model for Frank Martin's in "Where I'm Calling From." Ray had nowhere else to go. He had no money, couldn't pay the rent. He was so desperate for money that he took a job as clerk in the Tides bookstore in Sausalito, but he didn't stay there for more than a couple of weeks. His hunger for books ate up much of his salary. He never stopped reading, no matter how much he drank, and he'd bring home armloads of books. He quit that job and then hit rock bottom.

Maryann offered him the chance to go to Duffy's to dry out, almost the last chance to save his life. So she and Amy and I drove Ray up to Duffy's. And he was terrified. Terrified that he was going to die if he stopped drinking, or end up brain damaged from the seizures, the convulsions.

What a bind! Dead if you do and dead if you don't.

The doctors had given him six months and he'd be dead, maybe sooner. I remember when we checked him in at Duffy's, he was dead drunk. He'd been drinking all the way up as we drove through the Napa Valley, but after that first experience at Duffy's, we saw the turn begin to happen. He was there for about three weeks the first time. Then he got out of Duffy's –

He checked himself out of Duffy's?

As I remember it, he checked himself out, concerned about the money it cost, and also believing that he had learned enough about the disease of alcoholism that he could quit now. He went back and lived with Maryann for a brief period. That didn't work out, so he came to live with us. He didn't last long without a drink that first time. The personal and family problems, and the social pressure to drink – all his old buddies in San Francisco – it was just too much for him. He felt a desperate sadness over the breakup of his marriage. And the children were in trouble too. His daughter, in particular, was in deep trouble. I don't want to go into the details, but she's doing just fine now, and she has three beautiful daughters of her own.

What about his son?

Vance wasn't in any kind of physical trouble. But of course he was very emotionally wounded by the tremendous disarray in their lives. I had a great deal of sympathy for Chris and Vance, and I still do. Vance was really caught between. He had to finish high school, his parents were alcoholics, and his home had been yanked out from under him. He was a physically big young man, like his dad, and at times became violent with Maryann and Ray. He was so frustrated. He didn't really know what to do. Maryann was trying as hard as she could to keep him, both the kids, from going over the edge. This broke Ray's heart – to see the shape the children were in, to know the marriage was really gone. He started drinking again and moved back in with us.

You said something about him going to Duffy's for the first time. Did he go back?

He did finally go back to Duffy's but didn't stay long.

During the summer of '77 he'd gone off and started drinking again. Then he came to live with us again, but he'd learned at Duffy's how to taper himself off with reduced danger of seizures by having what he called "hummers."

Hummers? What are hummers?

Hummers are time-controlled shots of liquor. Ray had bottles of a kind of booze he hated to drink, the same kind they had given him at Duffy's. There was a time schedule. He'd start with a drink every half hour. Then a day later, you taper off to a shot every hour, then a day or two after that, one every two hours, then later every three hours, and so on.

What was Ray's hummer, the drink he hated most?

The cheapest possible bourbon. He gave the bottles to Amy and me, so he couldn't get at them, and he kept us on a schedule. Day after day, and night after night, we'd pour his hummers. I believe those days and nights were the lowest of the low he'd ever felt in his life. Sitting alone in our living room, sometimes in the dark, his marriage was gone, fearing he'd never write again, and that he had nothing. Whatever he owned – about one carload of books, manuscripts, a few personal items, some old clothing, a few artworks – had been packed in about six boxes and stored in the garage of the church next door.

All this happened even after the publication of Will You Please Be Quiet, Please? *Had he given up writing altogether?*

Yes. He thought this was as far as he would get. He said that more than once. One book and that was it. He knew he had to beat alcoholism first or his life was gone, he would die.

He'd been at our house a week, tapering off on his hummers and going to AA meetings at St. James Church. He looked out the window one morning and saw the church was having a bazaar. His few belongings had been spread out in the church-yard, ready to be sold. His manuscripts, his books, his few items of clothing, his artwork, whatever he had. So he and Amy and I had to go through the humiliation of going up to the ladies running the bazaar and saying, No, this is not for sale.

These are my belongings, there must be some mistake. Later we saw him sitting in our living room, all broken up, in grief, in tears. He has a poem in *Fires* called "Distress Sale" that captures those feelings.

Was this then the turning point?

He dried out in that apartment in San Francisco. This was after the second Duffy's Myrtledale experience, which he could no longer afford. So he had to do it on his own. When he was off all the hummers and completely dried out, he only hung around San Francisco for a few weeks before he went to the Southern Methodist Writers' Conference in Dallas, where he met Tess Gallagher for the first time. Although they both maintained that they didn't meet romantically there, seeds were sown for something to happen between them in the future.

What happened when he returned from the conference?

One of Ray's oldest friends, the writer Richard Day, helped him get a house up in McKinleyville, near where Day was teaching at Humboldt State, the college where Ray had received his B.A. He knew he had to get out of San Francisco, away from the people, places, and things that are discussed in the twelve-step program. I'm not sure, but Ray might have had one more bad time with drinking, just before he went up to McKinleyville and moved into this nice house. But he finally managed to stay sober up there.

Did he start writing again there?

He tried. He had a room all set up for writing. He wasn't writing very much, but he pulled off a great scam. He had written an outline for a novel which was something like the German side of the story told in *The African Queen,* and he had received an advance for the book idea from McGraw-Hill. I'm not sure he had every intention of writing the novel when he wrote the outline, but anybody could look at this outline and look at Ray's stories and wonder how in the world he was going to write that kind of book. He often joked years later that he was still getting notes every so often from McGraw-Hill asking how the novel was coming along. He'd tell them it was coming just fine. So I believe he used this money to get by on in McKinleyville, and there began a wonderful period of emerging from alcoholism, learning how to survive and be happy with sobriety. It is all very similar to the story "Chef's House." Maryann did go up and live with him that fall. In many ways they were like kids again. They went fishing every day, and played bingo, and visited old friends at Humboldt State. This was the real beginning of his recovery. He never had a drink again.

But they didn't live happily ever after, did they?

No, things fell apart because the children were in such terrible difficulty. His daughter, Chris, and her boyfriend again ran into some trouble with the law. All of Ray and Maryann's money had to go into bailing her out of her trouble. Chris came up to spend the holidays. Maryann worked as a waitress to make ends meet. Ray just couldn't be around all this, the family troubles, the guilt he felt that again they had no money. To keep himself sober, he had to get out and get away.

Where did he go from there?

He had a job to teach at the Goddard College program in Vermont, a two-week residency there, where he became good friends with Tobias Wolff and Richard Ford. Ray writes about this time in his essay "Friendship," and Tobias Wolff has remembered it vividly in his memoir about Ray. After that, I think Richard Ford set him up with a farmhouse somewhere in Illinois, but Ray couldn't stand the loneliness there, so he drove to Iowa City and moved into one of those tiny roadside cabins, a place called the Park Motel.

He had some money coming in from Goddard, and he also had some money he had borrowed from a student at Goddard. He was just barely getting by, really broke, living at the Park Motel, when Amy and me joined him. This time it was Amy and me landing on his doorstep. We had tried to make a life in New York City, I hoping to get a novel published, and Amy trying to find work again in the theater. It was one of the snowiest and coldest winters on record in New York. We went belly up. And as down to the bone as Ray was, he told us we were welcome to join him in Iowa City, where we all had old friends and could get jobs, and we could rent the little cabin next to his. This brings us up to the spring of '78.

Did Ray start writing again in Iowa City?

He was beginning to try to work again. Ray was always working in one sense, inside his head. But at that point, I don't think he had written a new story in five years. He was living at the Park Motel, and he was struggling to get his voice back, to find his way to writing again. What I do know is that the story "Why Don't You Dance?" and a story called "Hooks," later called "Viewfinder," came across the desk of the *Iowa Review* at that time. They accepted "Why Don't You Dance?" So these two stories, as far as I know, were the first stories he had written since emerging from his terrible struggle with alcoholism. At that point he was convinced that he had stopped drinking, and he was ready to put his life together again.

You were with him at the time?

Yes, surely. We were the down and out in-laws this time. At first we didn't even have the ten dollars a night to rent the cabin, and Ray lent it to us. It was all so much like typical early Carver country – tiny, seedy motel room, with a view out the back window of an even seedier-looking trailer park with strange goings-on day and night. Before that, just before we arrived, Maryann had come to Iowa City and they tried to patch things up for two or three weeks. Then a family emergency forced her to return to Washington. Ray rented an apartment in Iowa City, and Maryann moved back in again, one more try, and their son, Vance, also turned up that summer. Ray rented a second apartment to try to write in. Sometimes the whole family stayed in the houses where Amy and I had house-sitting jobs. It was a turbulent time. Ray called it "milling." We were milling around and getting nowhere. He was just emerging from his alcoholism, not quite a year sober yet. He left town for a while. Then Maryann left town, and him, and went back to California. Ray was pessimistic. One of his big concerns was if he'd be able to find a way to write again. He wasn't sure.

Was this about the time he landed the job in El Paso?

Yes, he had been offered a job teaching at the University of Texas–El Paso. That's where he went next. I had been in an auto accident that I couldn't pay for, so in addition to working a full day in the library, I took on a night job washing dishes in a restaurant. Ray came to say good-bye to me in the alley behind the restaurant. It was a sad time. He gave me one of his big bear hugs and told me not to give up. Then I watched him drive off with those few boxes of his things all packed into an old beat-up Oldsmobile.

How would you describe his feelings at this time?

Well, he was down to bare minimum, but he was going off to a new job. And at least he was sober, he had hope now that something would happen to him, but he wasn't by any means optimistic.

But he did stay sober after that, didn't he?

He did stay sober. He never had another drink. Even when on the way to El Paso, about a hundred miles out or so, his car broke down. He called Tess, who was also teaching there, and that's how they got together. He traded that car for a bicycle *(laughs)*. He traded it right on the spot. That's the way it was with Ray. Disaster happened. But he now had a great story he would tell about how he had once actually traded his car for a bicycle *(laughs)*.

Richard Ford

The stories seemed very fresh to me, and extremely gripping and dramatic. I thought they attempted to give language to things – to moments in life – which until you read his story, you never realized existed importantly. You knew they existed, but Ray made them hold a great deal – those moments. As with all great work, his stories made you pay attention to life.

Ford and his wife, Kristina, meet me at the door of their splendidly restored 1830s house on Bourbon Street in New

Orleans. They greet me warmly, hospitably. He has just arrived the previous day and is trying to recover from the effects of a six-day drive down from their other home in Montana.

It has taken over a year for Ford to agree to this meeting, and though he does his gracious best to make me comfortable, I have more than my usual measure of preinterview apprehension. He answers questions directly with no hesitation. A trace of southern drawl in his high tenor voice does little to deter him from speaking paragraphs at a time in rapid-fire bursts, with an earnest energy that later sparks off a touch of heat once or twice. When you talk Ray Carver and writing with Richard Ford, you're close to touching a piece of his heart.

Later in the evening, as we watch TV, I hear an astute running commentary from the author of *The Sportswriter* as Mike Tyson takes out an inept, frightened opponent in the first round. We all turn in early. The next morning, as we discuss the interview, Ford expresses uneasiness – a disapproval with what he perceives on my part as a latent quest for the sensational in a few of the questions. It's over, forget it, he'll not participate in this project.

A dark moment. Smooth sailing, and then here we run into an iceberg. I do what I can to control the damage, and we spend over an hour patching up the mess. There are a few weak areas that could stand amplification. Ford agrees to tape more questions and answers. After lunch, we watch a bit of pro football. When I leave, I know I've caught but a mere sighting of the exposed surface of Richard Ford. The massive remainder is kept well submerged.

When and where did you first meet Ray?
I first met Ray in November 1977 in Dallas, Texas. It was the same time that I met Tess, in fact. At the time I was a close friend of Michael Ryan, the poet. Michael was teaching at SMU and had asked me to be a part of the Southern Methodist University Writers' Festival. I had published one book and was barely out of the box.

Was that your first novel?
Yes, *A Piece of My Heart*. So I went, and Ray was there.

I hadn't any special anticipation of meeting him. I'd read some stories of his in *Esquire* and liked them. When I was in school in California in the late sixties, his name was around.

Will You Please Be Quiet, Please? *had come out by then. Had you read it?*

No. In fact I hadn't heard much about the book. At the time I wasn't leading much of what you might call a literary life. I was staying home writing. I wasn't paying much attention to the *New York Times*. The world seemed pretty big to me, as it still does. There were people out there writing, and I was happy to be among them. Ray had read some things of mine, or said he had. I think he may have read part of *A Piece of My Heart* which was published in *Esquire*.

Your book and Ray's book came out about the same time?

Yes, my book was published in '76 and Ray's book came out the same year. But we just hit it off. When we met, there was this sense of, here's a man I like. He was living at the time in Arcata and had been off of drinking for a while. I can never remember whether Ray went off the booze in June of '76 or '77. I know he hadn't been off it for long. There was an understanding among people around him that he had been a bad drinker, a provisional attitude having to do with how long he'd be able to hold off drinking. Indeed, when I met him, he hadn't had a drink in some good while, and he never did again that I'm aware. But he shared that provisional attitude – about himself. He was taking one day at a time.

So that was the beginning; how did it continue?

Yes, that was the beginning. We hit it off right from the start. I was living in Princeton at the time. And in the ensuing months we became friends. With other people – including Michael Ryan – I helped Ray get a job at Goddard. What I mean by help is that I vouched for him. Geoffrey Wolff I'm sure did too. We vouched on no surety except that we liked Ray and liked his stories, and that Ray would come to Goddard and teach and would not get drunk and disappear. Which indeed he didn't do. He came to Goddard and was a wonderful teacher and it all worked out fine. This was in January '78.

That was an all-star group up there that year. There was Carver and you and Toby and Geoffrey Wolff –

And Michael Ryan and John Irving and Craig Nova and Donald Hall and George Chambers and Robert Hass and Ellen Voigt and Louise Gluck – Of course that putative star quality is meaningless. I just think of those people as they were: my friends. And most still are.

How did you follow up with Ray after the session at Goddard?

After Goddard Ray came down to Princeton and stayed with Kristina and me for a week.

Is that when you got that farmhouse for him in Illinois?

No, I didn't get that place for him in Illinois. He got that himself. He got it from Curt Johnson, who published *December* magazine. Anyway, when he left Princeton he went to this house in Illinois. It seemed like a good idea to him. He wanted to write, and he seemed to have the drinking beaten. But he got out there and very quickly found he didn't want to stay. He hated it out there.

It was February and he was isolated.

He was isolated and felt cold as hell. As soon as he got out there the weather cracked down on him, and he left. I think of it now as being that provisional time. Still. He was a bit on the move, didn't have a lot of money. I think he and Maryann were separated, at least *de facto*. He was looking to be still in a place where he wouldn't get the willies. In retrospect, he was warding off the impulse to take a drink, I guess.

I believe that's when he returned to Iowa City.

That must have been when he stayed with Stephen Dobyns. I'm a third party to all that. But it was beginning to be clear that Ray was pulling himself together. He was working hard and writing stories. We talked on the phone often and he seemed utterly himself – by that I mean the way he always would be after that – cheerful, eager, generous.

*Regarding Maryann – did you have much contact
with her?*

Virtually none. They were separated at the time. At
least, I guess they were. I don't think they got divorced until
1982. They had been through a lot of travail together, and he
loved her very much, but they just hadn't been able to live with
each other any longer. He said that to me many times during
this period. However, Ray was the kind of guy that if there
was bad news floating around, he didn't tell it to you. He didn't
cry on your shoulder. In fact, he was quite secretive. I remember only once that Maryann called to say she was having that
birthday party for Ray, his fortieth, and could we come. But
we couldn't. I can't remember where that party might have
taken place.

You and Kristina?

Yes. Kristina and I were like a unit to Ray, and he took us
both on. There was a sense of mutuality, which was quite
sweet.

*Where did you pick up on him after he went back to
Iowa City?*

I think the next time was at Goddard for the summer session. I wasn't teaching there then, but I was there to give
a reading. Kristina and I had left Princeton and moved to
Pownal in Vermont. After Goddard, Ray spent a week with us.
From there he went out to Iowa City again, and that time he
was on his way to El Paso, where he had a teaching job. And
on his way down to El Paso, that was when the old car that
Vance had left him finally broke down completely.

*Down in Van Horn, Texas. The story he liked to tell was
that he traded it for a bicycle.*

(Laughs) You can bet that isn't true. Ray pedaling a bicycle, that would be the day. Unless the bicycle was on a track
to a doughnut shop.

Yeah, he probably just junked the car.

Sure, he junked it right there and never saw it again. He
took the bus on into El Paso. I was in touch with him a lot, particularly in the first semester in El Paso. I remember very

vividly talking him out of quitting his job at midyear. I remember him saying that he didn't like it there, and he didn't want to stay.

Was it because he didn't like teaching, or did he have other reasons?
I don't know. He just didn't like being there. It very well could have been that he had connected with Tess by that time and wanted to move up to Tempe. What went on between him and Tess between the fall of '77 and the fall of '78, I don't know.

A love affair?
A love affair, yes, but I wasn't privy to it. I just kept saying to him, look, don't quit this job. With this job, you can go on and get another better job. So don't quit it, because it will go hard for you if you don't stay in El Paso and you want to go someplace better. Indeed, by that time he was trying to get a job at Syracuse. George Elliott, who taught at Syracuse, loved Ray's work but was a little skittish of Ray because of his drinking past. I remember calling and telling George that Ray was a stand-up guy, and as soon as you meet him, you'll love him. And indeed when George did meet him, he took to him immediately, and Ray took to George, and they were great friends until George died.

So Ray went to Syracuse and set up his own little Mafia there.
(Laughs) Well, I don't know. But, if so, he was a very negligent Don.

(Laughs) No, somehow I can't see Ray as a Godfather.
No, Ray didn't enjoy teaching. He wanted to be writing.

But look at all his pals he brought in.
Yes, Tess and Toby and Doug, Stephen Dobyns. Hayden Carruth came at the same time Ray did.

Wasn't this about the time he'd got back to his writing?
Just before Ray went to Syracuse, he sent me a whole batch of stories in manuscript, about five I believe. These stories were written in sort of a spate, maybe even six stories. I

remember I didn't like a couple of them, or I had some things to say about them which weren't entirely praising.

Would it be fair to ask the names of those stories?
One was called "The Calm." I didn't like it very much.

Was that the one narrated in a small-town barber shop?
Yes. Anyway, I wrote him a long letter and told him all about it. Needless to say, there was a preponderance of praise too.

What was the other story?
I don't remember. This was in a bunch that included "Tell the Women We're Leaving." I had some critical things to say, but he'd sent me these stories and I thought he wanted some comment. So I told him some things, and he never showed me another story as long as he lived. *(Laughs)* Criticism – even of a friendly variety – was not what he wanted to hear at all.

Do you remember your criticism of "The Calm"?
Yeah. I was specific about "The Calm" because it was a story that had an envelope to its structure. The first-person narrator tells about another person's story.

A frame?
Yes, I didn't think the story had a closing frame on the backside. The story doesn't end outside the interior story, and I thought he should try that. Some sense of symmetry caused me to comment on it. I still feel the same way about it. For a while I needled Ray good-naturedly about that. Eventually he sent me the book, and I said that I liked it all but "The Calm." He'd always laugh and say I was wrong and that he'd received more praising letters about that story than any story he ever wrote. It became a joke between us. At first it wasn't a joke, but then it became a joke. He knew I loved his work. The story was published in the *Iowa Review.*

Ethan Canin told me that when he was editing the Iowa Review, *they printed a story of Ray's, leaving off the last line by error.*
What did they do about it?

I think they printed the last line in the next issue.
(Laughs) I'll bet that didn't bother Ray a bit!

Tobias Wolff

**People have taken this as a reference to Ray's own imminent death,
but in fact he wrote this essay ["Friendship"] before he knew he had
cancer, just as he wrote the story "Errand," about the death of
Chekhov, before he knew he had cancer. We are all dying. We should
all know that, but Ray knew it better than most.**

We meet in Wolff's hotel room in Miami. He is here to
give a reading at the annual Book Fair. He suggests that we
discuss the ground rules for the interview. I suggest breakfast
in the hotel coffee shop. The rules are established in a few minutes during our Florida Sunrise Breakfast Special. When we
return to his room I tell him how much I admired his tribute to
Ray in *Esquire* (September 1989). We discuss Ray's moving
little memoir, "Friendship" (*Granta* 25, Autumn 1988). He
passes on a couple of anecdotes about Ray and then tells me
how much he enjoys Miami – no other city like it in the world.
He draws the blinds open for a spectacular view of the bay and
ocean. It is a beautiful day.

In his essay "Friendship," published shortly after
his death, Carver writes on how he first met you and
Richard Ford, and how much he treasured the friend-
ship that grew from that meeting. There is a picture of
the three of you, and Carver writes, "Boy are these guys
having fun!" Later in the essay ". . . Things wind down.
Things do come to an end. People stop living. Chances
are that two of the three friends in this picture will have
to gaze upon the remains – the remains – of the third
friend, when that time comes. The thought is grievous,
and terrifying. But the only alternative to burying your
friends is that they will have to bury you." Could you
give us your sense of this piece?
I think it is a very interesting essay, full of a sense of

mortality, a meditation about death, about how death will eventually end this friendship. And people have taken this as a reference to Ray's own imminent death, but in fact he wrote this essay before he knew he had cancer, just as he wrote the story "Errand," about the death of Chekhov, before he knew he had cancer. We are all dying. We should all know that, but Ray knew it better than most.

My recollections are mostly the same as his, except that I actually did meet him before the time he mentions in the essay. I think it was dramatically convenient for Ray to use our meeting up in Vermont. He was drinking when we first met, and so I don't think he remembered it very well. We were out in Palo Alto at the same time back in 1976.

What were you doing there then?

I was teaching at Stanford, and he had been living in the area for a few years then. He was already among the best of the young writers around, even though he wasn't much known by the public at that time. He was still having a hard time placing his stories in literary magazines, because they were considered rather odd and old-fashioned, which they aren't, but were read that way because they weren't in the experimental mode of fiction that inhabits the pages of literary journals of ten years ago or so. I was very familiar with his work, and most of my friends were. We'd meet at parties, but he was a drunk at the time. He'd be funny, vibrant, but he wasn't very sensible to his surroundings. He was a different person later on. We really didn't get to know each other until the time he recounts in his essay and I recount in mine [*Esquire*, September 1989]. We only have certain moments in our lives when we can get to know a person well. These moments get fewer and fewer as we get older because of the demands of work and family. Ray and I had that opportunity in Vermont. This was like summer camp, winter camp. We were up there in Vermont in this dormitory for two weeks together. Both of us were night owls and we'd sit up and drink coffee and just talk all night like kids and it was wonderful. We got to know each other well. We did this for a couple of years – in each other's company for long periods of uninterrupted time.

Who were some of the other writers teaching there then?

Well, it was really an extraordinary place. Richard Ford was there, John Irving, Craig Nova, Stephen Dobyns, Michael Ryan, Ellen Voigt, Donald Hall, Louise Gluck, Robert Hass, many others.

What year was this?

These were the years '78 to '80.

After you began your friendship with him in Vermont, how did you keep in touch?

We were never really much out of touch after that. At that time, when we weren't in Vermont we were both in Arizona. He and Tess Gallagher were living in Tucson, and I was living with my wife, Catherine, in Phoenix. We used to exchange visits. When Ray started teaching in Syracuse, he suggested they hire me and Tess as well because they were putting their writing program back together again. It had been a very distinguished writing program, but a number of people had retired and died. From 1980 on we were all at Syracuse together. The Strauss Living award in 1984 allowed him to stop teaching, but he kept the house in Syracuse because Tess was still teaching there. We were in constant touch throughout the year. And he loved to talk on the phone. He was very boyish in that way. I notice this in my sons, this almost physical appetite for contact with their friends. You have that when you're young. It usually wanes when you get older, but Ray never lost it.

That's the way it comes across in "Friendship" – that you and he and Richard Ford are just good old buddies.

Well, that's the way he was. He was a buddy, and he liked having his buddies around him.

You must have struck a chord in him, because he couldn't possibly be like that with everybody.

No, he wasn't like that with everybody, but it was amazing to watch how quickly he made friends. He was a very sweet man, a very plain man, and he had a friendly feeling toward people. Let me give you an example. There's a poem of his called "Luck" about two boys at a house where a party is going on, and they get excited by the noise and the drinking. They go out and spend the night in the woods and come back the next morning and everyone's gone, the house is a shambles, and drinks are all around the house. The narrator, the poet, pours all the drinks together and says, "Friends, I thought this was living. A house where no one was home, and all I could drink." Notice the word "friends," the way he uses that word. With most writers, it would be an affectation, but it wasn't with him. That was his address to the world.

Geoffrey Wolff

Ray understands that questions and answers are in some way combative, and he mastered this understanding that every question is loaded in some way with menace and consequence. Every question seems to be binary. You have two roads you can go down, and the answer you choose can change your life. The smallest matters can have the gravest consequences.

I meet Geoffrey Wolff for the interview in his office at Brandeis University in Waltham, Massachusetts. It is a small room, about eight by ten feet, cement-block walls, one window, one desk, two chairs; bare and functional as a shoebox. A dozen or so photographs of Wolff's family and his boat are neatly displayed on a pair of wooden boards supported by hardware-store brackets meant to serve as bookshelves.

He is eating a tuna fish sandwich at his desk when I come in. He smiles and waves an arm in amiable greeting, and I see a remarkable physical resemblance to his brother Tobias. He is a cheerful man, intelligent, affable, and easy to talk to. We take turns passing on stories about Ray and his escapades. The conversation and ideas flow so spontaneously that I rush to hook up my tape recorder. I don't want to waste any of this good stuff, like a boxer leaving his fight in the gym.

Where and when did you first meet Ray Carver?

I met Ray for the first time in Vermont at the Goddard College M.F.A. writing program. It was very shortly after he had stopped drinking, and so it was the first job that he'd had after he had pulled himself together. We made an immediate friendship. The person who introduced me to him was my brother Toby, who had met Ray shortly before I did. I went to Goddard to give a reading and in no time at all we were laughing. Ray was a great laugher, and we sat around telling outrageous stories to each other.

Love at first sight. How do you account for it?

Ray was the first writer I had met who made me conscious that anything I said to him he would take as his property, and that was something I was perfectly willing to surrender for the pleasure of his company. So my first memory was of an extraordinary listener and an extraordinary user.

Was this in the winter of '78, the same time that your brother Toby wrote about in his wonderful memorial essay on Ray?

Yes, and there's a great story about Ray from that year. He was having a hard time financially just then. When he was given the Goddard job, a couple of his friends, Michael Ryan was one of them, had to make guaranties that Ray would be OK to teach and behave himself. Ray came ready to teach, though he was pretty shaky. He was in rough shape physically, but he had an atmosphere of resolve about him. As you know, each teacher at Goddard is assigned five students to supervise. Well, shortly after he left, it turned out that Ray had gone to some of his students and borrowed fifty to a hundred bucks from them. Paid it back too, which was a new habit for him.

You said that he'd take what you said as his property. Can you recall anything you said that became a Carver story?

Oh no. It wasn't a question of getting a story from me. It's a phrasing, a sense of observation, a kernel here and there. But of course we all do this. You don't know anything until you hear it. But with Ray, you were conscious of his attention, that he was making stories all the time, shaping them, figuring how to make them track. He loved to hear stories. I never knew anyone who was a better audience.

How was he at telling stories?

He could really tell a story. I remember he told a story once in Provincetown. He was in residency there, and I came to give a reading. I was there with Richard Ford and his wife, and my wife, and Ray was there with his son. Ray told us a story I had never heard before. It was about the time he was in Israel on a fellowship. He had his choice of Tel Aviv or Florence, Italy, but Tel Aviv paid five hundred dollars more, and that's all he needed to know. In the story, he put his kids in Hebrew-speaking schools that neither he nor they understood, and they lived in some squalid walk-up tenement, and he used to take a bus across town to buy fish. He'd come back on the bus with this bucket of fish. Well, the story was so graphic, it had art and geography in it. It had a character change, and motive, all ad hoc. And centered in this story was this bucket of fish on a crowded bus, and people staring at it. And the way the whole story started was somebody mentioned whitefish.

From what I hear, Ray was none too happy in Tel Aviv.

You see, I didn't meet Ray until after he stopped drinking, so all I know of his unhappiness was the great joy we all took in the narratives that came out of it. Ray had good luck. Ray had bad luck. He was an alchemist in the way he could turn the worst squalor into the best stories. So when I think of the bad old days for Ray, what I see are the wonderful stories.

How did you keep in touch with Ray?

We saw each other at Goddard, we corresponded. He came to see me and Richard Ford when I was teaching at Princeton. I saw him in Arizona with my brother Toby. We kept in touch, visited, and I was very much in touch with his work. I had the luck to be asked by the *New York Times* to review a collection of stories. I told them I had given up reviewing, but they said I might be interested in this book and they sent it on to me. It turned out to be *Will You Please Be Quiet, Please?* This was before I had met Ray. I saw those stories, and I don't think I was more than three sentences into the first story before I knew I was hearing a voice I had never heard before. So I was disposed to feel strongly about Ray before I met him.

Stephen Dobyns

*Are you another of those who first met Ray Carver
at Goddard?*

Yes, it was in January of '78. I was teaching then at the
Iowa Workshop and flew up to Goddard for the residency.

Had you heard of Carver before meeting him there?

Michael Ryan had been talking about him, and so had
Richard Ford. This was in Cambridge, where I was living before going to Iowa. Ryan had given me Ray's first book, *Will
You Please Be Quiet, Please?* and I loved those stories, so I
was eager to meet him at Goddard.

What was your impression of him when you did meet?

He was a big, bearlike guy. At that time I think he had
only stopped drinking for about six months and he was still
kind of fragile. Toby Wolff, Ray, and I became close right away.
We'd spend hours telling stories, staying up until three or four.

Was this your first meeting with Toby Wolff too?

Yes. Toby and I did a lot of cross-country skiing together
up there, and then we'd come back and talk to Ray. As I said,
he was still quite fragile. He was totally unready for the un-
comfortably cold weather, lots of snow and below zero. He had
a light pair of shoes and a jacket of some kind of vinyl, but he
was very good at, say, getting things. Like there was a guy
there who had a car, and after a couple of days Ray had the
keys for that car – then he had the use of the car – and by the
end of the residency it was as if it was his car. While most of us
had to walk through the snow getting around the campus, Ray
would always ride in his car.

Did he do any writing there?

I don't know, but he gave a reading of his story "Why
Don't You Dance?" and it was just astonishing to see the response to it. It was one of the things that made the program so
exciting. John Irving read a chapter of *Garp*, and there were
others. Listening to Ray read proved that he had what it
takes. Certainly, the end of that story lifts you right out of
your seat.

How did he get along up there in general?

He had a very rough survival, almost refugee, attitude toward the world. He'd never leave the lunchroom without taking a package of food, which he'd store in his room. Many of these packages would go untouched, but it seemed as if he expected to be cut off in some way or caught someplace without sustenance.

How did you follow up with him after Goddard?

He had no money. At the end of the residency I lent him a hundred dollars and he borrowed a hundred dollars from one of his students, and he took off for this abandoned farmhouse in Illinois someone had lent him.

How did he get out there?

He flew, but once he got out there he bought one of those what we called Okie cars, a '63 Olds or Buick. He phoned me and said the place was furnished entirely with lawn furniture, miles from the nearest town, freezing cold, and the moment he turned on the heat in the place all the flies woke up. So it was full of flies and his car wouldn't start up in the cold. He lasted out there maybe two weeks at the most and then called me in Iowa City and I invited him to stay with me. I was living within the city limits of Iowa City, but it was on a farm.

Were you teaching in the Iowa Writers' Workshop then?

Yes. I was living in a foreman's cottage on this farm and Ray came out, stayed with me, and slept on my couch. That fall I had canned a lot of applesauce, and Ray ate a load of pork chops with that applesauce.

Other than crashing at your place, what was he doing in Iowa City? Was he doing anything in the workshop?

No, no. He had his six students from Goddard that he had to keep up with through the mail, but he didn't stay at my place very long. He was trying to find a place to stay, and he ended up renting a room in a strange house where the owner had a weird double name like Sirhan Sirhan. He was an Arab but married to an American woman who was extremely anti-Semitic. Ray said the guy got him in there because he was hungry for conversation. The couple had a huge king-size bed, but she made her husband sleep on the floor next to the bed. Ray described how this Arab would lie in wait for Ray, eager to have a conversation. Ray couldn't stand it, and after about two weeks of this he moved out and came back to stay with me for a bit.

What was Ray using for money at this time?

He had a little coming in from the program at Goddard, but not much. I guess he owed the couple some rent money, because the guy kept calling me for the money. Then Ray got another place, and all this time his car was giving him trouble. It wouldn't start, and a number of times I had to go to a parking lot to try to get it going. Something to do with the generator. Some time before I had the same trouble with a car like that, where I'd take a hammer and tap the generator and it would suddenly start up. And of course Ray thought I was an absolute wizard. He was astonished.

Where was he living then?

He moved in and out of a couple of those rooms, and then Maryann came and they rented a kind of efficiency cottage outside of Iowa City in a motel.

Was this the Park Motel that they shared with Doug Unger and his wife?

Doug showed up with his wife, Amy. Ray felt a little disturbed about that. He wanted to devote his time to writing, then Maryann came, although he was glad about that. Then she became involved with an astrologer or a medium in a nearby town, which made Ray very uncomfortable. The idea of her talking to spirits and being involved with this astrologer unnerved him. Then the final thing for him was that the grandmother was going to come. That did it. He felt he wasn't going to have any time to write at all.

How long did that go on?

When he left Iowa City that summer, it was with the sense that he was escaping. He saw himself completely wrapped up in this situation that had complicated his life for years. That was the summer he met up with Tess. I guess he practically flung himself into her arms.

He had first met her the previous summer at the writer's conference at Southern Methodist in Dallas, hadn't he?
Yes, but in all the time I knew him in Iowa City, he never mentioned Tess.

Even though he was a great teller of stories?
Oh, he was a wonderful storyteller, but beyond that was his eagerness to hear other people's stories. A clear difference between him and Tess was that although she too is a good storyteller, she didn't like to give up the rostrum. Whereas if you told a story Ray would be right there saying, "Think of that!" over and over again. He'd say, "Gee! And then what happened? Gee! For crying out loud." In Iowa City that spring there'd be five or six of us sitting around till three in the morning telling stories and he'd wait for his turn.

I also heard some of that material turned up written in his stories.
Yes, you had to be careful around Ray. If it was a story you wanted to use, you simply couldn't tell it to him, because he sucked up everybody's stories. What astonished me, once I got to know Ray, was that no matter how peculiar his own short stories were, so many of them were based on fact. There were some he told that he never wrote as far as I know. Like the time he and Maryann were in court for bankruptcy and the opposing lawyer wanted to take their dog from them. He also told how he was hauled into court for collecting unemployment checks while teaching out in California. And how he and Maryann used to travel around making a few bucks cheating at bingo games, and afterwards the little old ladies would be chasing after them.

All that stuff was going on while he was still drinking. Hadn't he straightened out by the time you knew him?
Oh yes. We spent a lot of time together the summer of '78 at Goddard, and then when he came back in January '79. He was very helpful to me. My personal life was extremely complicated at that point. He would listen to me very carefully in a way you don't find in many people. Most people can't wait for you to finish so that they can start telling their own story. Ray

would listen and make suggestions. He was good at sorting through the mess. The following summer he came back to Goddard and Tess came with him. By that time he was living with Tess and full of stories about how much he hated Tucson.

He'd been off the booze for a couple of years by then, hadn't he?

Yes. He had written some wonderful stories while he was sobering up and before he was involved with Tess. Later it seemed to me she was trying to take too much credit for what he was doing. He was writing tons of poems in that spring and summer of '78 and showed me a manuscript he had prepared. We spent time going over them when we weren't discussing Chekhov. Later that fall, when I was teaching at a class in short stories at Boston University, I used Chekhov and Joyce and *Will You Please Be Quiet, Please?* as texts. My students were very good and I recall being almost disappointed when they showed a preference for Carver. Then that January 1979 at Goddard, Toby Wolff and Ray were teaching a class in Chekhov and I sat in on every class. Afterwards, the three of us would spend hours discussing the great Chekhov stories. Both Toby and Ray were almost obsessive about Chekhov.

Didn't he seem to be in better shape than he'd been the previous year up there?

Oh sure. There was a revolt by the women that winter against the so-called sexism at the residency. A number of things had come together to bring that on. Richard Ford had read the first chapter of his novel, *The Ultimate Good Luck*, which was in a different form than it was finally published. The first sentence of the novel was something like – There was nothing so-and-so liked better than to see two spics beat the shit out of each other. It also had a scene of a woman masturbating with a cake of soap in the shower while a man stared at her from outside her window. The dean of the college, a woman, stood up and protested, and other women protested. They were outraged. Ford grew very upset over this. Many discussions were held about the matter. Ford later revised much of the novel, and I think he made it a weaker novel because he was upset by this reaction to his work. This stuff just terrified Ray. He went immediately back in his room and tried to stay out of the whole business. The women were protesting, saying things like the men on the faculty preferred to hang out with the pretty women students. Toby Wolff had made the mistake that semester of teaching a class on pornography. It was a good class, but some of the women found much of it offensive. It all finally came to a hearing between the male faculty members and a number of representatives of this women's group. Toby indignantly said that he didn't spend two years in Vietnam to be chastised like this. Ray wanted no part of any of it. He was unnerved by it, as if somehow he'd be held accountable for this behavior.

He treats the women in his stories much kinder than he does the men. They are pained by the faults and defects of the men in their life.

I never saw anything in his work that could possibly be called sexism. He was amazingly gentle with women. He never did feel entirely comfortable with blacks, possibly because of what he perceived as their anger. He'd occasionally make remarks that would seem racist to me.

Like what?

Well, there was one he made a number of times. When he finally started getting requests for readings and job offers, he'd say, "This makes me feel just like a white man." I must have heard him say that half a dozen times.

There weren't too many black people in the small towns of Washington and northern California, and you don't find many in his stories. Offhand I can only recall the minor characters in the bar in "Vitamins," in the hospital in "A Small Good Thing," and in "Will You Please Be Quiet, Please?"

There's something curious about that. Clearly he comes out of a lower-class, blue-collar background himself, his mother and father were from the South, I believe Arkansas, which might account for some of these attitudes. I remember giving him a couple of books written by a black writer I admired, Ernest Gaines. He said he couldn't see anything in Gaines, he just couldn't respond to him.

How did Carver respond to criticism of his work?

He would listen to suggestions, but in the end it was his work, and he was extremely stubborn about this. Do you know Ray's story of the two guys picking up the girls and one of them kills the girls with a rock?

Yes. "Tell the Women We're Going."

Ray showed me that story, and I told him that I didn't like it, that I felt it didn't work. The whole violence seemed gratuitous. He was apologetic about it, but he stuck by the story. He had no idea where the story came from, and he felt an allegiance to that intuitive discovery, although he had no analytical sense of that story except that it had arrived. I believe he himself didn't like the story. Mostly, he had such a terror of things somehow getting out of control.

Do you mean he didn't like the story itself or its literary quality?

I believe he didn't like the violence in the story, but as for the literary quality, he felt the whole thing worked as a story. The language all worked exactly the way he wanted it to work, but the ideas of the story he would often see as something given to him, rather than something he'd made up himself, that he didn't choose them, but rather they chose him.

How about that strange little story of his about the couple quarreling over their baby until they literally tear it apart? And its weird title – "Popular Mechanics"?

Like many of his stories it turns into a metaphor, and it works in the way a poem works. It's an allegorical story about his children, and how the constant fighting between the parents destroys the child.

That's cutting pretty close to the bone, isn't it?

What always strikes me about his work, and it's even more apparent about the poetry, is how true he is to the emotion. You get this in a way from Ray's love of Chekhov.

Chekhov said that you have to write without any kind of constraint – any aesthetic or psychological constraint. You verify the emotion and that emotion is more important than what people might think of you because of the emotion, or whether the work will be published or anything like that. Your loyalty is to that emotion. Think of Ray's poem where he is looking for Baudelaire's grave in a Paris cemetery, and how his son and their guide keep trying to take him to the rock star Jim Morrison's grave instead. That poem is for me an image of Ray's ability to focus on what's most important in art, while the world itself is trying to distract you from that destination.

That's well put.

I spent a lot of time in Chile, going out to Isla Negra, where Neruda had lived, and I met this caretaker who allowed me to go around the house. Where Neruda worked he had three photographs. One of Whitman, one of Baudelaire, and one of Rimbaud. That's how it should be. You should always be close to the sources of your strength. And the writers who were important to Ray were like talismans whom he kept around him. *(Short break)*

Getting back to his poetry – are you familiar with his poem about Charles Bukowski?

I think it's a marvelous poem. I first saw it as part of a manuscript he had given me to read in the summer of '78. What mostly struck me right off about that poem was Ray's ability as a mimic. How much that becomes a skill of the writer. You could also say this of Chekhov, who was a fantastic mimic, and Ray wrote what seems just like a Bukowski poem. I had to ask him if he made it all up or did Bukowski really say those things. Ray made it up.

That poem sprung from way back when Ray was called on to escort Bukowski to a college reading. Can you imagine Ray as a designated driver?

(Laughs) He told me several times of going out to a restaurant with John Cheever about twenty-five miles from Iowa City. They both ended up drunk, and they thought it

would be a good idea just for the hell of it to walk the check. The plan was that Cheever was to go out to the car first, then Ray would join him and they'd drive off. So Cheever walks away and Ray sits at the table alone for a few minutes before he gets up and runs out of the restaurant. Ray said he shouldn't have run because all these waiters went chasing after him. He ran out the door with the waiters chasing him, expecting to see Cheever in the car, but Cheever wasn't there. The waiters grabbed him, and then Cheever comes walking out of the men's room. They finally got out of it once the waiters discovered they were professors at Iowa. They said it was okay, just send us the money. So both he and Cheever promised to send it to them. I asked Ray if he ever sent them the money, and he told me he never did.

I've heard so many of these horror stories about Carver, but they are always, like yours, told with such affection –
Here's another. That first time at Goddard in January '78. Ray walks into town for a haircut. It's a real small place. He comes back and his hair is astonishing. It's all ragged and terribly cut. I ask him where he got that awful haircut and he tells me this story about the barber. He's an old, old guy and this is his first day back at work. The guy had had a stroke. He could no longer cut hair with his right hand, and his left hand shook as he cut Ray's hair. Ray was afraid to hurt the guy's feelings, so he let him go on. Hell, I could have given him a better haircut.

You also told me the story of how he used to stash away food while he was there.
Yes, he used to take these packages of brownies and cookies out of the lunchroom, wrap them up in napkins, and take them back to his room. Once he told me, laughing, how he'd got back to his room and found that someone had swapped packages on him. Instead of finding six brownies, he found three pieces of stale bread. He thought that was the funniest thing in the world, that someone would play this trick on him.

Douglas Unger

Were you in touch with him while he was trying to sober up?

We'd spend time with him on major holidays. And we'd see him for four or five days at least four times a year generally. His attitude then was that he was slowly coming out of it, and he was trying to get back into his writing. In fact, he was writing the darkest stories he ever wrote, the stories in *What We Talk About When We Talk About Love*. He had reached such a depth of depression and also a stylistic minimalism beyond which I think it was almost impossible to go. I mean in stories such as "A Serious Talk" and "One More Thing." The very dark stories about the breakup of a marriage that are so stark and full of pessimism about the world. It was as though he was writing stories about people for whom the worst has already happened. What's on the page is really just an echo of events in the past which have destroyed the people before the story even begins. The dark death of love, and hope, and faith, and youth.

Where was he when he was writing those stories?

He worked on those stories in El Paso and in Syracuse when he got the job here. It was amazing to see the development in the work. He had discovered what I call a kind of *via negativa* of writing fiction. The style of the writing itself is a kind of argument from absence. He concentrated, in details and in describing events, on what is not there, or on what has not happened. It's as though the stories prove, in a way, that love and hope and charity and the finer human emotions must still exist, if only because of their striking absence for his characters after what they have lived through. It's just incredibly fine writing.

Could you expand on that, give us some examples?

Sure. You'll notice that most of his stories of this period begin with an assertion in the first few lines. Then that is immediately followed by a contradiction. Note how Christmas is described by what is missing or wrong or absent in the Christmas description in "A Serious Talk." Or the fact that the main assertion in the story is that a serious talk must happen between the main character and his wife, but of course the serious talk never happens. What I'm saying, I guess, is that Ray achieved a particular and extremely economical style by writing about what does not happen, by picking out what is missing, or by letting the reader know what should have happened for his characters but didn't. Even in certain choices of details you can see this. One example I like can be found in the story "Feathers." In the description of the house in the country, almost the only detail about it is the chimney. Then a point is made that there was no smoke coming out of it. Just choosing that one detail of absence somehow enables the reader to see everything that surrounds that one thing that is missing. Or take "Cathedral." The important detail about the visitor is the absence of his ability to see. That absence becomes spiritually the very gift of sight for the narrator. Do you see what I mean, or am I way off base? To my mind anyway, this *via negativa* seems to be at the core of Ray Carver's writing.

Was that much of a departure from his earlier stories?

One thing I know about Ray from reading his manuscripts and talking to him about his life was that some of his stories in *Will You Please Be Quiet, Please?* were around in some form or another from the time he was eighteen. His basic writing style didn't change all that much really. But in *What We Talk About When We Talk About Love* and some of the stories in *Cathedral* his writing took a very deliberate turn to an even more negative minimalist story. His style reached a stripped-down extreme beyond which I don't think he could or even wanted to go. He said in an interview once that he had to step back from that extreme style because he couldn't go farther. Later you can see how in some of the stories in *Cathedral* and the seven new stories in *Where I'm Calling From*, the fiction and the writing become more ample, broader, and actually allow love and hope and compassion to come in, to be a part of the story, to be there.

Ray wrote often about the importance of revision, how rewarding it was, how he actually liked to revise –
Ray had a fascinating attitude about his stories. I con-

sider it a liberating attitude for young writers. Sometimes he'd simply change a few elements of a story, or he'd add a frame to the story, maybe change character names. He'd send out the version he thought best. Years later he might send out the other version. Two similar stories with different titles might appear in different published collections. Ray had no qualms about this. After all, they were like different stories to him. And he didn't hesitate to reapproach his stories even after they were published and rework them. The best examples I can think of are "The Bath" and "A Small Good Thing." He viewed his work as a continuing process and was constantly revising not only manuscripts but even published stories. For instance, "Distance" and "Everything Stuck to Him." "Distance" has a frame. It's a story that looks back from a balcony in Italy, where the daughter has come to visit, and her father tells her the story of what he and his young wife went through one night when she was a baby, which is the same story as "Everything Stuck to Him." Ray had no trouble thinking of these as different stories and publishing them that way.

Ray's story "Intimacy," the story of a writer's visit to his ex-wife – as far as you know, did Ray make that visit?

I'm not sure that visit actually happened. But from personal experience, knowing both Ray and Maryann, I'm sure everything in that story had been said to Ray at one time or another. Ray and Maryann spoke often on the phone and wrote many letters back and forth. I know there is a tremendous sadness in Maryann now, and there has been for some time, about how the world, the literary media in particular, considers their relationship. She read all the reviews describing these down-and-out people in Ray's work, treating them like ragged lowlifes, most of them, saying how heartbreaking they are. Maryann is a proud, capable woman. She's an educated person, has a master's degree, and can quote from Jung and Blake and the major poets. She knows how hard she and Ray had it in the early days. She was his first sounding board. She helped edit all those early stories. She worked for nineteen years to keep Ray and the family together. Then to see their lives and his work so refracted and distorted to the world by critics, reviewers, and now even biographers, to see the most intimate portions of their lives shown in Ray's work treated that way, all of that really hurt her pride. And that's what "Intimacy" is about. It's the writer asking forgiveness for having allowed their lives to be so used and abused in his stories and by the world. Then of course the ironic twist of making use of that very apology as fresh meat for another story.

Are you saying this was Ray's way of seeking forgiveness, making amends? Or the route he took for another story?

No, life with Maryann was over, however much they still loved and cared for one another until his death. Ray was in love with Tess and was completely with her in his new life. He'd speak of the old life and the new life. The old life had a great many good things in it, but it ended with all the drinking and the bad old days and he'd never want to go back to that. I don't think he felt the need to ask forgiveness of anyone, not even Maryann. The new life was a life of acceptance, and all through this new life, he and Maryann were never enemies, never, no matter what happened. It's strange. She and Tess are so much alike. There are many differences, of course. But they're both, at heart, small-town Washington girls from working-class families. They're both literate, sensitive, self-made, and self-educated women, and both are incredibly strong and willful. Maybe I'm wrong, but I see them as similar in so many ways that Ray's deep love for one and then the other becomes totally comprehensible.

How did he react with you in his new life?

We were friends. We were family. We talked on the phone at least twice a month and visited each other often. I remember when *What We Talk About When We Talk About Love* was reviewed on the front page of the *New York Times Book Review*, Ray called up and said, "Did you see that? Would you believe it? Who would have thought it five years ago?" He was like a child at Christmas with every good review or piece of good news. He'd want to come over and play, share his gift, his success. He was astounded at the new reception of his stories. After so many years of rejection, the financial struggles, the drinking, even giving up writing, now when he least expected it the world embraced him. He never ceased to be amazed at that. What was happening, I believe, is that our culture finally caught up to Ray's style and subjects. The disillusionment of the seventies and eighties now suddenly found itself reflected in his work. Of course, he had been writing some of these stories since the sixties, or at least his basic style had been there all along. He was ahead of his time.

Was he able to enjoy this turnaround?

He was fascinated by it, and by the smallest kinds of pleasures it enabled him to enjoy. He'd check into a nice hotel room in New York. He'd laugh and quote his version of the Pinter line, "a person feels like he has a chance in a room like this." Just going out to dinner was a big occasion. And he'd always want to share this feeling with his friends. He was generous with his success. He helped so many other writers, his friends and his students. And in a literary way he was still growing. That was the most miraculous thing of all to him. Those years between Syracuse and Port Angeles were very productive.

How did Tess contribute to this new life?

Tess was instrumental in getting his life organized. From all the chaos of the past, Tess was able to step in and establish order, manage things so Ray wouldn't have to worry about bill collectors or other distractions, how to make ends meet, or how to find writing time. Tess would unplug the phone and put up a sign that said "No Visitors." Ray often said how happy they were. They were having fun together, too. Ray wrote the vast body of his work during this new life.

Ray wrote a great deal of poetry as well as fiction. How did he view his poetry?

I think writing poetry, more than fiction, was his first love. I don't believe that after Ray was turned down for financial aid as a young poet that year at Iowa that he ever gave up his youthful dream of being accepted by the world as a poet. Poetry more than fiction was an obsession for him. If he had a choice between writing a story or a poem – if writers really have that kind of choice – I think he'd favor the poem.

Is that why he wrote only poetry after he learned about his illness?

I couldn't say. But after he finished the manuscript for *Where I'm Calling From*, he and I had a talk about fiction and poetry. He wanted more than anything to complete another book of poems and was happy to be back to poetry. He was, I think, very noncalculating when it came to the impulses for his work. He wrote what he felt like writing. He followed his instincts and his own gut feelings about what to work on. I don't believe he ever violated that. When he completed the manuscript for *Where I'm Calling From*, he was also a little concerned. In this talk we had, he was feeling written out with his fiction. So he was naturally looking forward to getting back to his poems.

Was that before or after he knew he was ill?

This conversation definitely took place before he knew he was ill. I should explain that a lot of people kept urging him to write less poetry and more fiction. We were talking about that, and he told me that he wasn't sure if he had another story in him, that he had to fill his well again. I believe for Ray that always meant going back to writing poetry.

By that time he'd written "Errand," a distinct departure from his previous stories. Do you believe that was the direction his stories would have followed if he had continued in fiction?

He had a lot of fun with "Errand." I was at Yaddo when that story came out, and it so happened there was a copy of Henri Troyat's biography of Chekhov around. James Salter noticed that the death scene in the biography and a large part of the death scene in "Errand" were almost exactly alike, almost word for word. That caused quite a stir and discussion among the writers there.

Ray and I talked on the phone a day or two later. He told me that he had read the biography, was fascinated by it, and decided to use it when he got the idea for his story. To his mind it was no different from using parts of a story one of his friends had told him around the table. But it really is interesting that he used the primary text out of the biography and then turned it so completely into a Ray Carver story. He laughed at how someone had actually caught him at it, then said he might just do that same kind of story with the biographies of other writers he admired, like Maupassant, Dostoyevski, and Kafka.

So you saw a new departure in his later work?

The stories that broke him into something entirely new were "Blackbird Pie" and "Errand." I think "Blackbird Pie" is almost Nabokovian in its use of cryptic messages from the wife, a story at least partly about the interpretation of language. Ray was definitely playing with something different here. And "Errand," as I said, plays with the idea of writing a story based on the biography of another writer and making that story his own. I believe he might have been thinking of going off in those directions if he had lived long enough.

Which of his earlier stories were your favorites?

From the early work I'd choose "Neighbors" and "Are These Actual Miles?" Those two stories reflect to me the desperation of that time, and they are so beautifully crafted. "Neighbors" is a classic, a doppelgänger story, full of black humor that is characteristically Ray's.

Which of his later stories?

I'd have to say "Where I'm Calling From." It's certainly his most honest story. Ray was always honest in his fiction, that is to say that he was true to his personal vision of what is real and important in life. But that story goes a step beyond. Ray was revealing the depth of his own fear, his intense self-doubts, the ragged edge of his own recovery, and how precarious and tenuous recovery really was. To his mind, recovery from alcoholism may have indeed depended on luck alone. Ray was a great believer that he suddenly got lucky.

Geoffrey Wolff

What did you hear in Carver's voice?

First of all you can't talk about his fiction without talking about the speed of his beginnings. Ray propels you into his world fast, and without tricks. It's his absolute solid rock belief in the world he is describing, along with a master's understanding of voice. So you get propelled into his world sensually, and into the grammar of this world. Dumb-headed critics seem to pay attention to what kind of house Ray's people are living in, what kinds of clothes they're wearing, and all that. I don't think this has anything to do with his stories. They live by their sound, and syntax, his bravura abbreviation, the speed and indirection of the narrative. And in all these things, he is a great master of grammar.

Did you say grammar?

I say grammar rather than diction, because the *words* don't arrest or surprise me so much. It's their wonderful loopiness. I think Ray was able to make the same revolution in his own way that Harold Pinter made. For example, he understands questions, how they can be menacing. Ray understands that questions and answers are in some way combative, and he mastered this understanding that every question is loaded in some way with menace and consequence. Every question seems to be binary. You have two roads you can go down, and the answer you choose can change your life. The smallest matters can have the gravest consequences.

You mentioned the speed with which the reader is immediately propelled, I believe is the word you used, into a Carver story. Could that be because we understand so much of what has happened to the characters even before the story begins?

That's a good question. There's always something in the beginning that throws you a little off guard, because Ray was a master at locating a moment that would change people's lives.

Just to pursue this a little further. In the story "So Much Water So Close to Home," so much has happened before the story begins –

This is so, but they're all different. In "Gazebo," for example – that morning she pours Teachers over my belly and licks it off. And in "Viewfinder" – a man without hands came to the door to sell me a photograph of my house. In "What We

Talk About When We Talk About Love" – there's the slow unfolding of the story.

It wasn't only in his beginnings.

Yes, he's also a master of titles. And if he's somewhere now eavesdropping, I'm sure he won't mind my saying that he used to run a bit of a scam when he'd be asked to deliver a lecture on the craft of fiction. He used to have one that he'd pull out of his back pocket. It was a lecture on titles. He'd give a little rap on the importance of titles. He and I gave a team lecture once and he said, "When you see a house, the first thing you see is the roof, right? The roof is everything." Well, I looked at him and questioned whether that was the way it works. So he said, "OK, it's the chimney. The first goddamn thing you see is the chimney." When I questioned that, Ray said, "Well then, it's the front door. This is the title. You go through the front door and you're into your story."

Speaking of titles, and I may be stepping out of line here, I remember asking Ray to name his favorite short story. That's dumb-ass I know, but I asked it. He told me you could learn a lot from "Hills Like White Elephants," the Hemingway story. Maybe he was just dusting me off, but I read the story again, and when I came to the part where the girl says, "Will you please please please please please please please be quiet," I knew where Ray got his title.

Oh, if it was good, he'd take it from anywhere. In that story too there was something that Ray was a master of. He knew better than anyone where his characters should look. I don't mean point of view. I mean where their eyes fall, what they see and what they don't see. I think he learned a lot from "Hills Like White Elephants" when the characters look at each other, and away from each other, and at their hands, at their feet, at the table. Ray was a master of where eyes fall, where they rest. *(Pause)* Would you like to hear some fishing stories about Ray?

I've heard a few, but sure, tell me yours.

Well, I have two fish stories. One of them is from when my wife met him for the first time, she fell in love with him, everyone did, you'll hear that over and over again, that's the way he was. Anyway, her heart just opened to him. We were up in Vermont, and he said he was going out to do some fishing. She asked him if he were a fly fisherman. And he said that he was a fly fisherman if the fish were taking the fly, otherwise he used blasting caps. The other story is when my son and I and Tess and Ray were in Alaska together. We rented a car and went off to find a river where we could fish for Arctic grayling. In Vermont you only have to go a couple of miles to find a good trout stream, but we had to drive over forty miles to find a place to fish in Alaska. And when we got there, out in the boonies in Alaska, in the middle of the tundra, there must have been fifty or sixty cars there. Well, on top of that it was raining. Tess stayed in the car. She wasn't that stupid. But I was that stupid, and my son, Nicholas, and Ray were that stupid, so we got out of the car to fish. Ray was giving all kinds of instructions to Nicholas on fishing. And after awhile Nicholas got a bite. Ray started on Nicholas to pass over the rod to him. And Nicholas said that it was OK, he could handle it himself. But Ray kept after him and tried to take the rod, but Nicholas wouldn't let him. Pretty soon it was like Ray's story where they tear the baby apart.

He loved to see other people catch fish too. He always thought it was magic. Ray would say it like a litany, and you knew it was coming. "Goddamn it, aren't we lucky. Aren't we lucky," he'd say. He'd say it over catching a fish, or anything that happened. And in the years I knew him, he was lucky, he was blessed. I don't believe I ever saw anybody with such an alive awareness and appreciation of life.

What's your reaction to the criticism of him as
a minimalist?

I'll make one comment off the bat. The comment has been well considered, and the scholarly term for the comment is bullshit. I'm not sure I know what a minimalist is. I kind of think I know what people mean when they say they think they know what a minimalist is – that it is a taker-outer rather than a putter-inner. And to a certain degree, Ray was that. He liked to lean things down, but not always. He was certainly capable of being a putter-inner too. Ray wrote enough. It was a wonderful thing that Stanley Elkin, who is certainly no minimalist, said. He said that he didn't understand what this less is more crap was about. He said, "Less is less. More is more. And enough is enough." And Ray was someone who knew what enough was.

Now there was a time when the stories that are collected in *What We Talk About When We Talk About Love* were being screwed down, some of them, maybe a little too tight, you could say that, and I think Ray came to think this. As you know, when he revised those stories, he filled them out a bit, but I think not always wisely. I think "Mr. Coffee and Mr. Fixit," for example, in its leaner version is a better story than "Where Is Everyone?," the version he expanded and put in *Fires*. Certainly stories like "Cathedral" and "Errand" are not minimal. There are people who are tricksters, hacks, workshop writers who think they are imitating Carver in the way they were imitating Hemingway in an earlier time. They've created an atmosphere of sparseness and niggardliness, and there's no sense of life beneath the work. It's just lean and white space. But Ray wrote enough. His stories are full. As I say, there was a time when he was getting close to the edge, and in some instances not worth mentioning here he actually did go over that edge. Yes, he came close to crossing the line, as actually "Hills Like White Elephants" comes close to crossing that line. It could be argued that there is insufficient information in that story. But this minimalist crap is not worth talking about.

Robert Stone

He represents in a way a renewal of the American realist tradition . . . an inheritor of Hemingway, an inheritor of Sherwood Anderson . . . People will always want to read him to get an insight into the life and art of late-twentieth-century America.

This interview took place at the Rebel's Roost, a nineteenth-century guest house maintained by Sewanee University for visiting writers and lecturers. Stone was a guest there while running a two-week fiction workshop at the Sewanee Writers' Conference.

He did not express much enthusiasm when approached for the interview. He'd been interrogated countless times for book reviews and literary journals. He claimed he had nothing new to say, and every minute of his time at the conference had been spoken for. His card was full. Then, perhaps because he is basically a kind man, he thought he could squeeze me in Saturday morning, the last day of the conference, at nine. It turned out to be a bit too early in the morning for both of us.

Where did you first meet Ray?

I believe we first met in California some time in the sixties, or to put it another way, we were at the same party in San Francisco. I'd see him on odd occasions after that, but the first time I really got to know him was in Toronto at the Harbor Literary Festival they have every year. That was sometime in the eighties. We got to talk. Much more than people usually do at such conferences. I told him how much I admired his work. As I recall this took place at a historic restaurant, sort of a Williamsburg restoration that they took us to.

After that . . .

After that I saw him at his house in Port Angeles a couple of times. We went fishing together. He had a boat. One year when we were fishing, we got lost in the fog. We had a really good time. Ray had a manner that was very much his own, a kind of shambling and colorful manner of viewing things. There was something incongruous about him out there in his boat. We caught a lot of salmon and had a very good time. I don't remember much else that happened that particular time. I was staying with him.

I remember Tess and I drinking some great single-malt scotch, I drinking most of it. Raymond had been on the wagon for years and years. Funny, that's all I remember from that time, the boat and the single-malt scotch.

That boat. Lenny Michaels remembers Ray wondering just what the hell he was doing out on that boat when he could be home writing. Did you recognize that?

Yes. He had a relationship with the boat that was always ambiguous, and Raymond was the master of ambiguity.

Ambiguity? Ray Carver?

Well, highly impacted. Ambiguous in the sense that you don't always know exactly what a character is feeling. Or to put it in another way – his characters give you the impression of experiencing a number of different things at one time. I think you can call that ambiguity.

You mentioned that Ray was on the wagon, but we know he wrote many fine stories before he gave up alcohol. How do you think that affected his writing?

Well, all I know is that he thought it did. I know being an alcoholic is a great disrupter of energy, and he wrote with a great burst of energy after he stopped drinking. Anyway, that's what he used to say. I don't know where the cutoff point is in terms of his stories. I know it must have made a difference. He believed it did.

Was it Cheever who said he could always detect a line written by a drinking author? Something like that. Could Carver or any writer turn out good stuff while drinking?

I don't know. It's not possible for me to write while intoxicated. There are people who do it. I mean it's not like it hasn't been done. Fitzgerald, according to what we read, wrote with a bottle. I don't think it's terribly uncommon, but in terms of a short story I can't do it.

You had read Carver before you met him?

Oh yes, I had read some of his stories before, but more after I had met him.

Could you tell much difference between the stories he wrote before he stopped drinking compared to the ones he wrote afterward?

I'm afraid I can't tell you much about that. I'm not too familiar with when he wrote what, so I couldn't say which of his stories he wrote before he stopped drinking.

Let's try something else. Which of his stories do you consider most characteristically Carver's?

Yes, the one where the guy occupies his neighbor's apartment while he's gone on a trip. I believe it's called "Neighbors." I loved that story. I think that so represents Carver.

What's your opinion of his last story, "Errands," about the death of Chekhov?
It was quite different. Like he was about to enter a whole new phase. I understand that Tess found many stories in his files after he was gone.

When I asked Tobias Wolff which story he considered most characteristically Carver's, he cited a poem called "The Baker." What do you think of Carver's poetry?
I like it very much. I think Raymond was working toward a kind of refining of his vision, and as his stories became more and more accomplished, he began to compress even more. He found certain things that he was expressing so succinctly that they became poetry.

In the last few months of his life, he wrote no stories, only poetry. What was your sense of that?
I admired his poetry very much. I think he was going to be – he *is* – a major American poet.

In your estimation, where do you believe Carver's work will stand in American literature?
I think his work will stand very highly as a successor. I mean he represents in a way a renewal of the American realist tradition. He is an inheritor of Hemingway, an inheritor of Sherwood Anderson. His work is very good and very rewarding. People will always want to read him to get an insight into the life and art of late-twentieth-century America. He has an international reputation. I think he will stand high.

Carver's experience and life seem to be in every page he wrote. As his friend, as well as fellow writer, could you comment on that?
To a certain extent his life and work did combine. I had a great affection for Carver. While we lived on opposite sides of the country, we were friends. He had personal qualities that were reflected in his work, a certain kind of excellence, generosity, perceptiveness. He cared about people. His writing

was very much the way he was. You could admire and love the man in the same way you could love and admire the writing.

That recalls the passage in Catcher in the Rye *where Holden Caulfield talks about books that when you finish reading, you wish the author was a terrific friend and you could phone him whenever you felt like it.*

Something like that. Sometimes you'd meet the man and it would be disappointing, but in the case of Carver it wouldn't be.

His poem "My Boat" conveys that open spirit and friendship to one and all.

The man was very much like his work.

Can you recall the circumstance where you first heard of his fatal illness?

I had heard from others that he was ill. Then one night I was standing behind him at the Literary Lions night at the New York Public Library where everyone dresses up in a tuxedo. I slapped him on the back, and when he turned around I could see he had lost an enormous amount of weight. That's when I saw that he was really very ill. I remember being very alarmed and shocked at the way he looked.

It is tragic that there will never be another Carver story.

It's a great loss. The premature death of an artist of such stature. A great loss.

Jay McInerney

Right up to the very end, he seemed flabbergasted by each new honor. I remember he once called me to tell me that the *New York Times* was going to do a profile on him. He said, "Can you believe it, the *New York Times*?" Well of course I believed it. Anybody would. I changed my whole life to follow him to Syracuse, hardly at the top of my list of favorite places to live if Ray wasn't there. He was considered one of our greatest writers, but he was constantly amazed at the high regard in which people held his work.

When I asked McInerney for the interview, he readily agreed, no questions asked. As I recall, his reply was something like, If it's for Ray, I'm for it. We set up an appointment easily, with no jockeying around. It took place in the living room of his recently remodeled Greenwich Village house four days after I first phoned him. I tell him that I believe "Raymond Carver: A Still, Small Voice," (*New York Times Book Review*, August 6, 1989), the memoir of his days at Syracuse with Ray, was a fine piece of writing. He is glad that the piece has been so well received, as Ray had been such a positive force in his life.

*Did you meet Ray before you were his student
at Syracuse?*

I first met him here in New York. Oddly enough, I opened the door of my apartment in Greenwich Village and standing there was Raymond Carver, who at that time was my favorite writer. It wasn't quite as coincidental and weird as that. In fact, my friend Gary Fisketjon, my current editor, was working at that time as an editor at Random House. Gary was a friend of Gordon Lish, who worked at Knopf. Well, one day Ray Carver came to town to give a reading at Columbia, and Gary and Gordon had lunch with Carver. After lunch they both had meetings and work to attend to, and Ray didn't really have much to do. So Gary called me up and asked me if I could take Ray around and maybe show him the city.

Had you been published at that time?

No. I knew Gary from Williams, where we had become best friends. He was just starting out as an editor at that time. So he called me up, this was actually the day that John Lennon died.

That would make it in the winter of '80.

Yes, around that. Gary asked me if I wanted to meet Carver. I thought he was kidding and I hung up on him. He called me back and said, No, seriously, Carver is coming to your house. And within moments there was a knock on my door, and there was this giant bear of a man in my door frame.

I recognized him at once as Carver and welcomed him in. The idea, I guess, was that I should take him sightseeing or something, occupy him for four or five hours.

And how did you do that?

Well, we just sat down and started talking about one thing or another, mainly about books and writing, and we never got out of the apartment. The time just flew. Then Richard Ford came by. He was a friend of Ray's. It was the first time I had met him. We all had a wonderful time talking, and the next thing we knew it was time for Ray's reading at Columbia, and Gary came to pick him up.

How did you follow this up?

After that I wrote Ray a letter telling him how happy I was to meet him. I was surprised when he wrote me right back. We started a correspondence and subsequently when he came to New York he'd visit with me and Gary. We started to become friends.

Were you working on your novel at that time?

At that time I was working on a novel that I never finished and some short stories. When I met Ray I was just basically trying to support myself as a free-lance writer doing research writing, book reviews, and it wasn't easy. That was one of the things Ray recognized when we corresponded.

What was that?

He said if I really wanted to make it as a serious writer, commit myself to the act of writing fiction, I would have to arrange my life accordingly. He felt that living in New York and having to support myself in the most expensive city in the country was draining away a lot of my energy. After about a year of this I was just numb. He suggested I consider coming up to Syracuse to study with him.

Why do you believe he did that?

Well, there were two aspects to his interest in having me come up there. One being that he felt that my devoting two years to learning how to write fiction was a good idea. And he felt New York was a crazy place for me –

He wasn't too far off there –

No, he wasn't. I'm still amazed he took the time to encourage me, because I had some resistance. I still felt I was in the center of the media and publishing world. Sometimes it's easy to confuse that with, you know, the literary world. The literary world exists wherever there are writers and wherever there is a man or a woman alone in a room writing. That's the literary world, and I was a little foolish in confusing the one thing with the other.

How did you settle that confusion?

Carver nudged me along with the idea of graduate school. For me the idea of graduate school didn't make much sense unless I would study with a writer I greatly admired. To me Carver was the best writer going, so I applied for graduate school and received a fellowship, which enabled me more or less to afford to live.

Ray must have been behind that.

I imagine he had a lot to do with that, and subsequently he helped me find an apartment, so in the fall of '79 I moved up to Syracuse, about half a block away from Ray and not too far away from Tobias Wolff.

How did you do up there?

I think what Ray did for me really changed my life. I think it's quite possible that if I hadn't met Ray I would have gone down the wrong road. I'd be an editor of a magazine today, or something like that, which is not to say there's anything dishonorable with that, but one thing Ray did for me was to pound away at the idea that the only way to be a good writer was to write every day. Sometimes he'd even call me up, if he hadn't seen me, and ask, Did you write today?

Did he follow his own advice?

I remember many years later as a joke calling him to ask if he'd written that day, and he said, No, you have to write every day until you *are* a writer, then you can take a day off every now and then.

So do you now take a day off every now and then?

(Laughs) I take days off. On the other hand, Ray was the first one to teach me that writing well is a lot of hard work and you can't be afraid to sit down every day and pound away at it. Even if, and especially if, it is not coming well.

Was Ray your mentor, your only teacher there?

I was enrolled in the program, I guess it was for an M.A., but my primary interest was to study with Ray and to have time to write. Everything else was a bit of an annoyance. But I also had the added bonus of Tobias Wolff, who was an excellent teacher, an important writer, a good squash player, and a great guy there as well.

But was Ray your primary influence?

Both men were very important to my development, but I suppose Ray was my mentor. Long before I'd met him, his work had inspired me. Subsequently he did spend a lot of time with me. I could always bring him a story. He'd go over it with me.

Even if you weren't enrolled in a class of his?

Yes. That was the nice thing about it. I think Ray felt the same way. The whole classroom structure was an annoyance to him too. He didn't particularly like teaching, standing up in front of a class. He was a very modest man.

How was he one-on-one?

Oh, when he'd take a manuscript and red pencil it, there's no doubt he had authority. He could always take a story and make it better. He was an excellent line editor. He was a great coaxer of stories; whatever was there that was any good, he would find it.

How would he treat a bad story?

He was never harsh. His criticisms were roundabout. The worst thing Ray would say about a story was, I'm glad you got that behind you. What he meant by that was there was no further point writing the ninth draft of that story. Eight was enough to get it out of your system, and you didn't have to go back to it anymore. He was willing to indulge you and that was about the harshest thing I ever heard him say.

How else did he motivate you?

He was also my mentor in the sense that he was the first writer who encouraged me, made me feel I had talent. I looked up to him. I wanted to be somehow a writer in the same way that he was a writer. I wanted to learn by example.

Did you?

You know I'd thought that writing was something that took place between drinking bouts, or travels to exotic lands, or between your seventh and eighth marriage. That was certainly one prominent model of the writer in America. Ray taught me the real job was sitting down every day and, as he said, putting black on white. That was very inspiring.

What more did you learn from him?

Well, you know he'd been through so much by the time I met him, and he'd come out the other side. He insisted that what he'd been through had only distracted him from writing. I think his writing improved as he sobered up, so he was also a steadying influence on my life in giving me a model of the writer that wasn't a self-destructing meteor.

Like . . . ?

Let's face it. Like most of the more conspicuous American writers were and are.

Getting back to Ray. You said that you saw him as not very comfortable in the role of teacher.

Ray was somewhat an unwilling teacher. That is to say, he was so modest, he almost didn't trust himself to give advice. I think he believed it a peculiar fate that led him to be a teacher. He thought it strange that so many American writers supported themselves by teaching. On the other hand, he thought it was better than sweeping floors or pumping gas, which he had done in the past.

Those who were close to him have commented that he regarded his success as an unexpected gift, as if he was getting away with something. Did you notice that?

That was an endearing trait of Ray's. Right up to the very end, he seemed flabbergasted by each new honor. I remember he once called me to tell me that the *New York Times* was going to do a profile on him. He said, "Can you believe it, the *New York Times?*" Well of course I believed it. Anybody would. I changed my whole life to follow him to Syracuse, hardly at the top of my list of favorite places to live if Ray wasn't there. He was considered one of our greatest writers, but he was constantly amazed at the high regard in which people held his work.

You've said that you have high regard for his stories. But beyond that, what do you see in his work?

One of the things that hasn't been mentioned enough is that each of his major collections represented a different stage in his development. That was not frequently noticed. People kept discovering him, as if he'd just been born. That is to say, even the *New York Times* review of his second book, *What We Talk About When We Talk About Love*, was actually a review of his first book. And so we were disappointed that the reviewer treated it all as one lump.

This collection, What We Talk About When We Talk About Love. *Wasn't this the one where the stories seem pared down to a bare minimum?*

Yes, this was the collection that fixed a stereotyped image of minimalism to his work. The collection went very far in exploring how much can be left out in a story – the old Hemingway notion. In fact, so much was left out that Ray subsequently published these stories in their original and to me more satisfying longer versions.

Do you find his earlier work preferable to his later?

I wouldn't pick one period over another. To me it's remarkable to see the continuity *and* the development. That is to say, by the time Ray published his first book, he knew what he was doing. I suppose nothing could have the impact on me as *Will You Please Be Quiet, Please?* because it was like a bolt out of the blue. For some of us it must have been like picking up *In Our Time* for the first time. Suddenly this very new language, this wonderful new idiom. It's the world as you always suspected, but you never realized it was until you read the book. It had an incredible impact, and I suppose I'll always love that book, especially as it hit me so hard.

Which of his stories would you call typical of his early work?

One of the earlier stories typifies some of the ways Ray felt about fiction. "Put Yourself in My Shoes" is very much what Ray said fiction is all about. It was the first story I heard him read at Columbia on the night that I met him. When I first read the story, I felt the menace in it. Like much of his work it has an edge of darkness. But when I heard Ray read it, what came through was the humor. The effect his reading had on the audience was remarkable. It was remarkable in the way you felt impelled to laugh at some of the most awkward moments. I think he liked that and thought it was not an inappropriate response to his work.

Which of his later stories would you single out?

So many people discovered Carver in his later work like "Cathedral." It's an interesting story for me because I heard him tell it so many times before he wrote it down. It was fascinating to see it develop. The first time I went to Syracuse I stayed with Ray and Tess. Ray told me of the visit of the blind friend of Tess. It was a very funny story. At the time I didn't hear anything of the cathedral or the television show. It was just a series of funny stories that Ray was telling on himself about his own discomfort having to be around this blind man. Ray was a quirky guy, full of idiosyncrasies that all his friends could mimic. He made fun of them himself, both on and off the page.

What did you think of "Cathedral" when you read the book?

Something remarkable happens in that story that usually doesn't happen in a Carver story. It has a different kind of ending. The ending of a usual Carver story leaves you on the brink of an abyss, and you look down into it. In "Cathedral" it's more like you're looking up to the sky and the sun is coming out. It's an unusual story for Ray in many ways, and I think he was proud of it for that reason.

It is an unusual Carver story. Where did you see a difference besides the ending?

In "Cathedral" as well as in "A Small Good Thing" there was perhaps a new emphasis, a compassion for how we have to deal with each other. Which is not to say the stories are better or worse. Ray was sensitive to the charge of middlebrow critics that his work was consistently depressing. In "Cathedral" he was saying that although life is tragic, perhaps once in awhile you can beat the odds.

As you say, Ray received his share of adverse criticism, and you are certainly no stranger to the form. Would you care to comment about bad reviews?

Well, I wouldn't want to equate Ray's with my rap. I think he did take a few bad raps. One of the things I learned from reading Ray's critics, and knowing his work as I did, is how often even our best literature is caricatured. And how even a writer as widely admired as Ray is so often misunderstood, even when he is being praised. He got a lot of satisfaction from his press, although he was often bewildered when he read about himself. I guess ultimately he thought, Well OK, if it's good we'll take it to the bank and not worry too much about it. But this minimalist thing always bothered him. Ray wrote the way that he wrote, and he felt it was a belittling term. He didn't believe his work was any more minimalistic than anyone else's. I remember three bad reviews that Ray received and he never forgot them.

Could you tell us?

I don't want any names here because these people are still around. I told Ray I'd get them sooner or later. *(Laughter)* Naaah, by getting them I mean to say that someday I would let it be known that the reviews were wrong and spiteful. I'm saying that it's altogether too easy for critics to forget that there's a person at the other end of the work. I did see Ray hurt by a few reviews, but on the other hand I don't think many writers have been as highly regarded and appreciated in their lifetime as was Ray. Overall I'd say it was a joy to see so good a writer so well appreciated. On balance I'd say that Ray felt he was really blessed, and he was blessed. Even though some of us felt frustrated by what we considered to be the awkwardness and stupidities of some of the more casual criticism.

When I queried Toby Wolff about this, he said something to the effect that perhaps we should all be so lucky as to be considered the head of the column to be attacked.

(Laughs) Well, Ray was such an unlikely leader. I think Ray was much too modest to realize how widespread an influence he was. I mean, you look at all the short story writers younger than Ray, and there's hardly one that you might say didn't come out of Carver's overcoat. I'm sure Ray was not aware how influential he was. One year I was a reader for an anthology of short stories put out by Random House called the *Random Review*, which didn't last very long. I had to read all the literary magazines to pick out the year's best, and that was the year when just about every story in those literary magazines was an imitation of a Carver story. It was astonishing how many people were trying to write like him, myself included.

His work seems so simple until you sit down and try to do it.

It's impossible to do it the way he did it. The best you can do is learn from it and develop your own voice and style from it, as so many have who started out as Carver disciples. There's an extended family of writers who were so touched by his work that they feel like they were his friends.

Maryann Carver

Ray's story "Intimacy." What was your reaction to the emotion and sentiment expressed by the narrator to his ex-wife, begging her forgiveness?

It's difficult to say. *(Pause)* The truth of it is I loved Ray Carver – first, last, and always. From the moment I met him until right now. There's no ending to that ever – and he felt the same about me. I learned from Ray. I knew how to live it unconsciously, but I learned as a concept from Ray what unconditional love really is. He'd say, "I love you whether you're good or bad." And indeed he did. And I loved him whether he was good or bad, even though there's no doubt I went through absolutely incredible grief over him. For years afterward I was truly heartbroken.

In modern psychological terms you're forced to say that no one hurts you. You allow someone to hurt you, and therefore you have to take responsibility for your own feelings. From that criteria, I can't say that he hurt me, although for years I felt he did. I did not feel I had a real choice about whether or not I was going to be hurt. It was a visceral response that almost overwhelmed me. God knows, and I am beginning to, he had his share of grief and suffering too, despite the fame and fortune that came to him.

I was in so deep in that relationship, and he was too, that pat clichés don't cut it. We'd been in it forever. I met the love of my life when I was fourteen years old, for God's sake; and it takes a story like "Intimacy" to say what the psychologists merely hint at. Our emotions were so real, and raw, and overwhelming, we strongly affected each other always, together or apart.

What was your reaction to his success when it finally came?

After *Will You Please Be Quiet, Please?* was nominated for the National Book Award, and all those reviews came out in *Newsweek* and *Time* and all the press, it was a shock to me. Of course, it was exactly all that we had always prayed for, what we had worked so hard for, sacrificed for, but the fact of the matter was that it was tough to read those reviews and see your lives held up and analyzed. Characters were called inarticulate members of the working class, involved in violence and doomed to go nowhere. And again there was such a mix-up between what is your real life and what is fiction because he did have he and she and their two children, a boy and a girl, over and over again in those stories. I found these classifications very difficult, because I had such great pride in Ray and his work, and the hard work I had done and the things I had accomplished.

We had become beautiful people. We had developed before the great fall into people of enormous style and promise. We were also good people, hospitable and charitable people. All our friends came and stayed with us. Our families came. We believed in Homeric hospitality. We worked hard and it did pay off. All of a sudden, after many years of struggle, we did own a lovely home. We were both teachers. We did have enough income. Then when everything was in place and the great challenge was gone, all that we had worked so hard for was knocked down. *(Pause)*

You were saying that all you had worked for had been knocked down –
I read that book again with new eyes after all the reviews came out. I felt as if I were in a fishbowl and yet not really seen. Life was different than it had been before anybody knew us, and our lives had not been held up to review. Ray, of course, could not be blamed for what reviewers said; and I had always loved everything he wrote, starting with the first love poem he ever wrote for me. I always knew he was going to be a great writer, and I insisted on that. All the time he was drinking, I'd tell him that it would be the worst catastrophe that could ever happen if he ended up as a second-rate writer, because we always agreed that he would be up there with the very, very best.

But convoluted as all this difficult part is, after the reviews, drunkenness, tensions, and separation, I then would read many of Ray's stories and poems, especially the later ones, with a very thin skin when I'd see how the lady or the son and daughter were done in for his capital gain. When *Fires* came out, for example, one of my son's professors was so concerned for him, knowing him to be a hard-working student and affable person, that he took Vance to lunch and tried to comfort him and explain what poetic license was all about. The kids, God bless them, have wonderful senses of humor and absolutely adored their father, again whether he was bad or good.

I know Ray did what he needed to do to write captivating stories and poems; profit, personal catharsis, and hurt to family members were secondary considerations at best. It is just that privately he was so decent and loyal. When he'd talk to me on the phone or write me letters, he would treat me with the utmost respect and love. I was the mother of the children, and if they needed anything, we worked on it together. We were a family, an unusually close family, all of us being basically as sensitive as flowers. So if anything came out in print that was less than complimentary, less than real or true, I'd be very hurt and shocked by what felt like a real betrayal. Yet we'd both long before given up our personal selves for his literature. I had to lose my life to gain my life, so to speak. Looked at one way, Lenny Michaels was right. We did pay for those stories with our lives. Ray is dead, and I've lost my identity.

And about that story "Intimacy," God bless Ray. He wrote whatever came to him, and if he could use anything, he did. I became supersensitive as to how I was depicted on the page. But now as I look back, I see Ray did not hesitate to portray himself either, in any position, humiliating or not. But he was a man and could get away with it better. He was also a star. He had a voice. I truly have been quiet, thank you. After all, what does it matter if Ray Carver humiliates himself? He doesn't really. He is Ray Carver.

May I say that whenever he wrote about the woman who may be construed as you, it never seemed to me to be condescending in any way.

Thank you. I didn't used to think so. I never did when we were together. I could read between the lines. He was captivated by me, first, last, and always. He used to say to me that I was absolutely dazzling. And anything negative, even in the last works, well, one knows, in my heart of hearts, he did protest too much.

I read him as sympathetic to nearly all the women in his stories. They seem to be suffering for the shortcomings of their men.

Yes, Ray loved and understood women, and women loved him. Women know when a man really cherishes them or is just on a macho pursuit. Ray was sympathetic and lovable, and women adored him.

Dick Day

Could you define what you find remarkable in his work?
If you take one of his really early stories, "Furious Seasons," you'll find it a little bit like an experiment in Faulkner. It's a melodramatic story and Ray has to figure some way to hide the melodrama, so he tells everything that happens in the present in the past tense, and everything that's in the past is told in the present tense. He puts that slight dislocation between the reader and the story, which makes it just a little difficult to know what happened. That is a highly sophisticated technique, as sophisticated as anything he did in his later work.

A definite change we see in Ray's work comes between his beginning with very tight, very spare stories and an opening out as in "Cathedral." I wrote him a letter right after that story appeared. I said it was the only story he had written in which a character transcended his condition. I thought it to be the best story that Ray had written at that point. He was leaping off the page, away from his normal mode.

Then there is his last story, the smooth, elegant story, "Errand." Ray studied Chekhov, reading all his stories, his letters, the biographies. He understood the emphasis Chekhov placed on finding the precise detail. Ray wrote the story, I think, for Chekhov and focused on the waiter and that champagne cork. He dealt with the death of a writer he loved and amazingly did it in that writer's own manner. There's the death of the master taking place in that hotel room, but what do you see? You see the waiter, the champagne cork. It's a story that Chekhov would have loved.

In those early stories, and in much of his later work, there is a sometimes overt, sometimes unspoken astonishment at what happens in life, at the often ominous unfolding of events, and at the strange, destructive things that people can say and do. That astonishment, central to the voice of his narrators, stayed with Ray in his life as well, stayed through big troubles with alcohol and divorce, and then increased in the good times when, sober and with Tess Gallagher as his companion, he was recognized, honored, and paid good money for his work.

William Kittredge

You mentioned that "Where I'm Calling From" is closely autobiographical. Of course that could be said of almost all of Ray's stories, and he received a few knocks for that. Could you comment on that?

I believe every writer discovers the story that's theirs in a way. For a long time, the story that Ray discovered – early on, I think "A Student's Life" was the first one of any consequence – was Ray and Maryann, Ray and Maryann for a long time. One of the things his friends knew and could point out from story to story to story, and Ray was perfectly willing to tell you, was that this is the thing that happened, this is where I got that story.

She was not his only source, was she?

No, not the only. I remember Ray and me sitting at a bar in Missoula when a woman bartender told us about being arrested the night before, because she and her boyfriend got stoned and moved all their furniture out on the lawn, set up lights and all. After a while the neighbors got annoyed and called the cops. I looked at Ray and told him that had to be his. So he wrote it, changed it a little. The one about the guy moving all his stuff out in the driveway for a yard sale.

"Shall We Dance?"

Yeah, years later, but mostly he found stories in his life. Then in the transition, when he was quitting the booze, I don't know, because I wasn't with him in the sense of seeing him all the time, I don't know where those stories came from. Like "Cathedral," which I presume came from experiences he and Tess had.

Yes. Tess once worked with a blind man in Seattle.

Seems like it. So he continued to use autobiographical material. I think he had very clear standards that he learned very early on. One of the books I remember in his library in the house in Cupertino was marked up, scribbled all over. It was a college textbook on double stories. You know, Dostoyevski's story "The Double" and that story by Henry James, and all those other doppelgänger stories. There was a book he had used in college, maybe in a class with John Gardner. One of the things that struck me about those stories was the way they were like Ray's. Sort of put yourself in my shoes or try my blindness. They were stories that encouraged you to somehow put yourself in someone else's situation imaginatively and thereby generate compassion for them. I believe Ray formed these ideas about storytelling from the very start, way back at Chico State.

Ray made fictional references to Maryann in many stories and poems, and in his essay in Fires *he writes openly of the hard years he and Maryann shared. From your perspective, how do you see her affecting his writing?*

Maryann is a person I admired a lot, and I still do, although I think she is to a degree wounded by the things that have happened. But when I knew them, she was the one that kept them together. Ray was the one who stayed home and didn't hold jobs. When I first met him, he was working for SRA in Palo Alto. He soon lost that job and stayed home the next year and wrote while Maryann worked. She taught school over in Los Altos, and there was an endless kind of chaos surging around them.

But it was a mutual decision. She agreed that Ray should stay home and write while she worked. She didn't resent that, did she?

Oh no. She supported him and supported him all the way. She was an extremely intelligent woman. She critiqued his stories. They talked about them. They did interesting things together. They clearly had a mutual agenda that had to do with his work. She would support him, and that was great. It was a mutual understanding that it would all come to something good, but at the same time it was also somehow very fragile. There was a hell of a lot of drinking going on, and a lot of chaos, unfortunate things during those years that led to a sense of betrayal on both their parts. It was as though this contract had been fractured and healed up, and fractured and healed up, over and over again. So many times that when they

147

finally broke up, Ray told me, "There's been too much water gone under the bridge." I remember his exact words.

Referring to that time, Lenny Michaels said, "They paid for all those stories with their lives."

He's exactly correct. They took risks constantly, risks with their emotional security. They lived on the edge all the time. They stayed out there, and I really think it was a conscious decision on their part to live on those edges, to court experiences.

How did you keep in touch with him after he stopped drinking? Say after '76.

Less and less. We'd write back and forth. Then he went to El Paso, and then Tucson, where Tess was teaching. He got a Guggenheim and shortly after that he got the job at Syracuse, and then he and Tess really got together. So it was much less handy to see him. We'd get together maybe once or twice a year. He'd come to Missoula occasionally to give a reading.

Did he seem any different from the old days?

Well, I was sober and I could see this guy trying to look at the world again, and get his ducks in a row, and figure out who he was and how he wanted to comport himself in the world. You could just see him growing, becoming more generous, more open with people, and more reasonable.

Did he ever backslide? Flashes of the old Ray?

Of course there were still elements of his behavior that were eccentric, just being old Ray, but there was always the warmth. But I could see him become more capable in reacting with the world, and the world began to come to him in ways it never did before.

That must have been a hell of an adjustment.

One of the things that interest me, and it's true, is how much he and Dick Hugo were in so many ways alike. They both were guys writing from a kind of disenfranchisement, some sense of not being part of the major world. Writing was a way of justifying your life and celebrating things that didn't seem properly celebrated. At some point in their careers they began to be properly recognized. They began to have some success. And I think both of them had trouble for a while with that success, because it was a real change in self-image. They had seen themselves as failures, as people who lived on the margins of things. They both reacted for a while as though saying, if you think I'm terrific, then watch this.

How do you mean?

Oh, they'd be invited to read at Yale or somewhere, and they'd immediately get drunk for two weeks, as if to deny they were this terrific guy who got invited to Yale. It was, I think in lots of ways, a fear of success, a fear of becoming someone else. Someone who negotiated with the world well and easily. And I think at some point after McKinleyville, some point probably with Tess, Ray turned that corner and realized who he was. He wasn't being false to that other person he once was. He could do all these things and still keep that compassion and generosity. I think the same thing happened to Hugo, but he fell back after awhile. When he died, he was drinking heavily again.

That fear of becoming someone else is close to what Lenny Michaels told me about Ray saying that whenever he was out on that boat of his he couldn't help wondering why the hell he wasn't home writing – where he belonged.

Oh yes, he could be more ironic than that. He'd look at me once in awhile and say, "Are we getting away with it or what?" Something like that. Like look at me, here I am, a guy with a boat! At the same time, he was very attached to it. He loved having all those things. One of the last times I saw him was in Seattle, almost at the same place where we first met. This was just before he got sick. It was at a celebration for Dick Hugo about November '87. Ray and Tess were staying at a posh hotel near the Market, and Ray was talking about why didn't he and I get together and buy a condo near the Market overlooking the harbor in Seattle and so forth. I don't know where the hell he thought I'd get the money for it, but he was clearly enjoying his success at the time, embracing and having fun with it. On the other hand, not taking it too seriously. He was never obnoxious about it.

But you knew he was enjoying every minute of it?

Oh yes. Why wouldn't he? After all, he was a saw filer's son from Yakima, and he worked hard, and all these things finally came to him. He got them by himself.

How would you describe Ray's sentiment about Maryann after their separation, after his Bad Raymond days, after he had become successful?

It became difficult for Ray after the separation. He knew he owed her a great debt, and he clearly did in anyone's eyes. She had kept his life together for years and years. She'd helped him imaginatively. They'd been entwined in an emotional compact about getting the work done, and she was clearly portrayed in many of those stories in all kinds of unflattering ways. It didn't bother her at all, at least as far as I could ever tell. It's just so sad that after a long series of emotional betrayals of various kinds, great anger developed. It got so that they couldn't be in the same room together essentially. Ray felt great sadness, but it made his life impossible to live, impossible to work, impossible for him to do the things he felt he had to do. At the same time he was so aware of the great debt he owed her. It was a bind for Ray. He knew he had to do his work, but back there all the time was somebody he had left behind.

In one of Ray's later stories, "Intimacy," he depicts a writer who shares many of the feelings you have just described. This fictional writer visits his ex-wife ostensibly to seek perhaps forgiveness. Do you view that story as a sort of payback?

Of course you never know, but I'd have to say it's a depiction of part of his feelings at least. He felt terrific guilt and sorrow, and he felt something valuable had been lost. He also felt that in the nature of their compact, he was the one who had walked away with all the skills. Like two people in a contract, and one gets to leave with all the success, and the other gets to stand out in the rain. And in a way that is what happened, and

Ray felt, as anybody would, great guilt over it. Though I must say I never heard him talk about it in that way, but we both understood it wasn't a thing we would talk about. Of course, you never knew with Ray. In the early days he'd used her so ruthlessly in those stories, and so maybe this was just his way of getting another story. Or maybe it was his way of paying back, probably some of both for all we know. I don't think it was "I'm going to make you a gift of this story." Again I think he took his own guilt, his own life, his own deepest feelings and used them to make art out of it in ways that were partly a payment back to Maryann and at the same time another story.

There's a poem about her in Ray's last book before he died. He seemed to be more generous to her in his poetry than in his fiction.

I've noticed that in his poetry too, at least five or six times.

There's a story there.

I don't know how she feels. I saw her once in Seattle about a year ago. We spoke for about two minutes. It was a strange situation. I was at the University of Washington giving a reading of a piece I had written about Ray after his death. I had no idea she was in the audience. Afterward she came up and she seemed to be very touched and pleased about the piece. We were very friendly for a few minutes, then she just turned and out the door she went. It was the only contact I've had with her in ten years.

And there's another story. Do you have any favorites among Ray's stories?

Well, "A Small Good Thing," "Cathedral," maybe the revised version of "Will You Please Be Quiet, Please?" I don't know, there are maybe twenty of them, but those are the titles that stand out offhand.

What did you think of his later work?

Well, that story "Intimacy" we were talking about, I don't know, I'm not so sold on that story. I thought "Where I'm Calling From" a great story. I really loved "Errands," about the death of Chekhov. And this may be an aside from your question, but I think Ray was very deliberately changing his art when he died. That's the reason for all those poems. I think that's the reason he was recharging, exploring, looking for new directions. He had explored the old orientation as far as he wanted to. I think he was, as a major artist will, trying to enlarge his scope, onto a larger stage. He was feeling his way, and these were all kind of studies toward what he'd begin to do had he not died.

He described how he loved to revise his stories, even those you've mentioned as his best pieces.

I think those longer versions of those stories of his like "A Small Good Thing" were really his masterworks. There is a significant difference in the stories as they appeared in *What We Talk About When We Talk About Love* and later versions. For instance, William Abrams, in his introduction to the O. Henry collection in which "A Small Good Thing" was the leading story, said something like, Wasn't it courageous of Ray to take a brief story from his previous book and enlarge it this way? Well, the fact is it was just the opposite. He had written the story, but his editor Gordon Lish had cut it down to the short version. The short version of that story is enormously diminished in its emotional power. It's no coincidence that Ray changed contractual agreements, changed editors and all that. As he told me afterward, "They can't change a comma from now on."

What's your reaction to all this talk of minimalism?

I don't think of Ray in terms of being minimalist. I don't think he was an emotional minimalist at all. He was dealing with what was at least for me major emotions. When I reflect and see my own life in the mirror of some of those great stories, like at the end of "A Small Good Thing," these stories are consistently telling me I must learn to be good, to be humane, compassionate, considerate of other people. That is a major emotional orientation and, I think it's utterly important to say, absolutely political. I think Ray had a very sure sense of his politics. He was simply saying, we have to be more compassionate, we have to be more considerate of each other. Ray said that over and over again in major ways in all those stories.

Tobias Wolff

Ray's last published story, "Errand," about the death of
Chekhov, that you mentioned earlier has a far different
style from any of his previous stories. Do you believe
this represents a change of direction in his work?

Well, as you'll notice in the story, he comes back to what is
very characteristic of his writing – the experience of an ordinary person, the waiter, in an extraordinary circumstance. He
doesn't know what is happening and his life is illuminated by
something he cannot fathom. He's carrying the burden of history for a moment. It seems to me that Ray's interest in the
end was almost more with this guy than it was with Chekhov.
Whether or not this story represents a change of direction in
his work, I can't say. I rather think not, because of the other
stories he was writing at the time like "Blackbird Pie" and
"Who's Been Sleeping in This Bed" and "Elephant." I don't
think his work would have changed so much in that he would
have written about historical figures, but there is a change in
the spirit of his stories. His earlier work is hard-edged and exact, and there isn't very much of what I'd call the spirit of kindness in the voice, though I love those stories still. I still read
his stories of that period. They remind me of *Dubliners*. They
have that same detachment, but later on there's a moderation
in the tone, a gentleness, a spiritual restlessness, and a pro-
found compassion for the people he's writing about. That's the
way I see his work – I don't want to use the term developing
because it seems to suggest that one thing is preferable over
the other. It isn't, it's just different, but his work was changing.

I always found it interesting to read the latest Carver story,
because it was always going to be a little different from the
last one. I remember reading "Cathedral" for the first time. I
was lying on a couch, and I had the feeling when I came to the
end of that story that I was levitating. Literally, of course, I
wasn't, but I felt like I was levitating. I was so charged by the
story and drawn up by it that I ran to the phone and spent
about half an hour trying to track Ray down. I finally found
him at Yaddo, and I had to tell him at that moment what he'd

done. I just wanted him to hear from another writer what a masterpiece he had written. I can't think of too many times when I've read work that made me want to do that.

Is there any single piece of his that you prefer over the others? A favorite story or poem perhaps?

I can't really do that. I loved so much of his work. That's the thing about Ray – he was never not himself. I can't think of a story of his that doesn't bring him sharply into my mind. I have many favorites, but among the favorites I cannot make any distinction. I love "Cathedral." I love "A Small Good Thing."

Which version of "A Small Good Thing?"

Not the short version, the one called "The Bath." That was actually the only story he wrote that I didn't like. When it came out in his collection *What We Talk About When We Talk About Love*, I didn't care for it at all, but I loved what he did to it later in "A Small Good Thing." There's "Feathers," and the stories in his first collection that I still treasure like "We're Not Your Husband" and "The Idea" and "Put Yourself in My Shoes," many others.

And "So Much Water So Close to Home" . . .

When I start naming my favorite Carver story, what's going to happen is I will name them all.

Do you find his poems very much like his stories?

The voice is the same, but the poems are more personal than the stories.

If you won't single out a story or poem of Ray's as your favorite, could you perhaps recall a scene or section that stands out in your mind as characteristically Carver's?

He has a poem called "The Baker" that I've always thought of as something very, how can I put it – I felt that Ray's heart was right there in that poem, and his wisdom, and his experience of life. It's about a baker in Mexico who lives in a little town where Ray invents a meeting between Count Vronsky, Anna Karenina's lover, who is acting as a mercenary in the Mexican revolution, and Pancho Villa. They meet at the baker's house. They both become interested in his wife, and she's sitting in Pancho Villa's lap and kissing him on the ear. They're talking about women and horses and getting drunker and drunker with their pistols out. The poor baker is terrified, and in the morning when he gets up and they're asleep, he takes his shoes and sneaks out of the house. At the end Ray says that "this baker, humiliated, terrified, running for his life, he is the hero of this poem." That goes to the heart of Ray's sense of life, that rejection of the heroic and lofty. The virtue of endurance, just staying alive in this world. Ray honors that in his work. Poetry gives Ray the chance to speak directly. He speaks in another way in his stories, metaphorically you might say. The stories are equivalents of some condition he wants to write about.

In the story "Are These Actual Miles?," when Leo sends his wife out to sell the car and he's walking around the house and he's even thinking about hanging himself, Ray writes that "Leo understood that he was willing to be dead." That's such a devastating line to read. There's no way of articulating that condition without having felt it. Then in "Cathedral," the scene when he has that blind man's hand and he's guiding it through the motions . . . Scene after scene comes back to me.

Though I know Ray's work very well, in the end it's very difficult for me to isolate moments. He is not a particularly quotable writer. That's one of his virtues, that he never tried to achieve a beautiful line. It's the steadiness and quietness of his prose that creates his sense of reality. You never get the feeling, Oh yeah, the writer got off a good one there. That's never in his work. I can read things that are more brilliant on the surface, but they don't go to the heart of things the way Ray's work does. He gets there in a very quiet, unassuming way, but he's only apparently simple. It takes art to do what he does.

So much of what he writes seems drawn from
his experience. In "Vitamins," for instance . . .
Why do you say you know that really happened to him?

Are you turning this around?
No, I get to ask questions too. Why did you say that?

*I'd say because it's written so well, so true. Not
journalistic, but the details are there, and the feeling,
and the humiliation of the man. You can't just
imagine these.*

Well, suppose I tell you that this didn't happen to Ray.

*Then I would have to say that if it didn't happen to him,
then it had to happen to someone he knew very well.*

Are you talking about the literal circumstances of the
story? You see, I think you have to make a distinction between
his work and his life. Ray was an artist. He was a creator, not
a self-biographer. He used elements of his life in his work, but
he didn't simply transcribe them. This is not an autobiographical story. What is autobiographical in this story is the spiritual
condition that he describes of humiliation and fear and moral
drift. That's what's real in the story, otherwise it's a fiction. A
good writer should make you feel as if he lived the story he is
telling. But at the end of the story, we always have to draw
back and say, This was a story. If it were a memoir, Ray would
have called it a memoir. When people immediately assume his
work was autobiographical, it takes something away from his
artistic achievement. It is an artistic achievement to make
someone feel they have had an encounter with reality, when
what they have had an encounter with is a writer's imagination. I mean, look at Ray's story "Night School" in his first collection. There again we have the feeling of somebody telling
something he actually did, but that's not in fact the case. That
is a made-up story. So you have to be very careful about at-
tributing to Ray experiences he wrote about, simply because
he wrote about them so well. This is an important point, because people often talk this way about Ray's work, as if it were
all simply his life story. He certainly would use anything – he'd
use things from my life, he'd use things from Tess's life, from
his friends' lives without any scruple at all, as well as from his
own, but he wasn't writing his own biography.

*As in the story "Elephant," where the narrator tells of
his family members sponging on him?*

There may be things in there that are autobiographical,
but they aren't in the end the story.

156 Tobias Wolff

And in "Intimacy" where the narrator goes back to talk with his ex-wife. Did that happen?

It may have happened in his mind. I'll bet a lot of these things happened in Ray's mind, but that's as real as anything else. The big thing is that the stories are authentic. They are real stories, and whether or not they happened exactly in that way to him, well, who cares? If we want to know what happened to him, we can always find out, because he was never shy about telling us. He wrote about his life in the essay "Fires." He wrote about it in his memoir of his father. He wrote about it in his poetry.

Then he would use his experience for his art without coloring it?

Of course he colored it. He was an artist. He colored everything.

What do you mean by coloring?

When you simply transcribe reality, it isn't real anymore. You get the Watergate tapes. You get something without any continuity or substance. That's why when people try to write they find it so difficult. They think, I'll just put this down the way it happened. But there's something missing. And it is exactly that coloration that Ray brings to his writing. He has a take on the world. The things that happened to him are not just set down. They're organized according to the way he sees life; his vision of life colors everything he wrote. So it isn't passed on as a neutral transcription of experience. It is individualistic, personal, subjective. That's what I mean by colored, but please note that it's your word, not mine.

I suppose if there is some heat in my response, it is because I am sensitive to hearing Ray spoken of simply as a man who wrote about his own hard life. That is not why his fiction is so powerful. I've read many stories of hard lives and they generally leave me cold. I am unmoved because they have not been turned into art. The private becomes public in the realm of art, and unless it can be turned into art it remains private. That's what Ray was able to accomplish. He was a great artist, a great artist.

Then those critical of his work misunderstand this?

I think so. I believe they don't make a distinction between the life and the work. They don't make a distinction between the man and the artist. He was an artist. Like most writers, Ray was not above cultivating a certain myth about himself, and that may contribute somewhat to the way people read his life into his stories. The fact of the matter is, they are different things. I would like to see Ray regarded as the great artist he was, and not as somebody who had a terrible life that he wrote about.

Hasn't he become the focus of the attack on minimalism or the so-called K-Mart fiction?

That's true. He has been a lightning rod drawing that criticism. Well, we should all be so lucky as to be considered the head of the column to be attacked. First of all I don't think he ever used the word K-Mart in any of his fiction. *(Pause)* You know, I'm not going to dignify this by discussing it. I just find this whole minimalism thing, or as it's called in England, dirty realism, a perversely uninteresting way of reading. It's a way of talking about writers without reading them carefully is what it really is. The minute you start talking about other people as though they were one, you know you're in trouble, and that goes for writers as well. I don't like categories. They talk about the Moderns. They talk about Joyce, they talk about Fitzgerald and Faulkner and Hemingway using that term. What the hell do they have to do with each other? I mean really, they're all completely different, and the only thing they have in common is they lived in about the same time. They teach courses on the Moderns in the universities, so no doubt someday they'll teach courses on the Minimalists, and that will be just as stupid.

What do you believe Ray's position will be in literature?

Well, first of all anything I say on this is obviously complete speculation because we don't ever know what will happen. But I have a strong suspicion that Ray will be one of those writers who will be read with care and love as long as people read our language. He has penetrated a secret about us and brought it to the light, and he does it again and again. You have to go to the water and drink. There's something pure and cool and honest in his vision of life and the beauty of his language, its exactness, its cadences, and its music. People will go back to it again and again and again.

Richard Ford

When you say you loved his work, what is there in the work that you love?

The stories seemed very fresh to me, and extremely gripping and dramatic. I thought they attempted to give language to things, to moments in life, which until you read his story you never realized existed importantly. You knew they existed, but Ray made them *hold* a great deal – those moments. As with all great work, his stories made you pay close attention to life.

Was that what made it a Carver story?

I suppose. He would tell you something, and then he'd tell you something else, and then he'd tell you something else. And every time he'd go to the next, to the next, to the next. It was surprising, dramatic, extremely informative emotionally. As soon as you realized what he'd told you, you realized the great hazardous possibility of overlooking those things: in ordinary life moments, small events, utterances; and that for our humanity to survive they needed to be observed. The other thing I loved about his work is that I thought it was very funny. *Very* funny. I've seen him give readings of the story "What We Talk About When We Talk About Love," and there's a moment there when the character makes a noise like a bee, "b-zzzz b-zzzz." I've heard Ray read that story aloud and start laughing. Again, he managed to do what great writing does, to deliver the fullest array of human response to complicated life. In that way it was often very instructive work.

When you say he inspired laughter in his readings –
He made *himself* laugh, as well as his listeners.

That may be, but I once attended a reading of "Intimacy" –
You know, I said to him after I read that story, "Jesus,

Ray," I said, "I read your story about Maryann." That's very unlike me. It's unlike me because I recognize and I insist in my own work that direct correlations between life and what gets represented in stories are impossible, untrue. And I didn't even know Maryann, but this remark just leapt out of my mouth. I said, "I read the story about Maryann." And he said in a very guarded way, "That wasn't about Maryann." And then I thought to myself after I said that, well, that's right. Even if it's not right, it's right.

Could you clear that up for me?

Well, I really knew practically nothing, certainly nothing more than what he told me about their life, his and Maryann's, or about the time they spent together after they were divorced. I don't know anything at all about that. I had no reason to think it was about Maryann, except that the story was so authentic sounding.

Didn't it ring true to everything you'd heard about him and Maryann?

It rang true to everything I knew about Ray. *(Laughs)*

Do you think Ray wrote that story with humorous intent?

I don't know. I would say that if that story originated in anything like what it represents to be, that when the original events were taking place there was no humor in it. When he wrote it, though – Ray was a very astute craftsman of his stories and authored every effect, so I can't believe that he didn't know there were many funny things in this story.

You know, Ray seemed in many ways like a natural. And to a certain extent, he was kind of a natural. But he was also scrupulous and thoughtful and careful and knew literature from the heart, from the gut, as well as from the mind. What he loved, he loved intensely, and studied intensely, so I believe he could only know every ramifying effect of his stories.

What you've just said makes me think of the line in "Intimacy," where after being raked over the coals by his ex-wife the narrator says, "Make no mistake, I feel I'm home."

I think that's one of the balming effects of his work. His

stories always seem to talk about grave things, but there's always something that you can take away with a sense of benefit. Not a message, but just something you can use.

There's one story of his that always bothers me, "Popular Mechanics." What's that story all about?
What's the last line? "In this manner the issue was decided." As to what that's all about, there's only one person who could've answered that.

Ray's last story, "Errand" – I thought I could always recognize a Ray Carver story.
You can't, though. By which I don't mean that you can't sometimes recognize a story of his by its, quote, style. But you couldn't *always* do it. He could surprise you. His work, his style, changed. That's an unfortunate thing about the terms Carver country or Carveresque as a putative literary description. Most of the sightings that people took on Ray's style – by which I mean particularly the length and cadence of his sentences, the length of his stories – those sightings mostly are from *Will You Please Be Quiet, Please?*, his first book.

Do you believe they are overlooking his later work?
Well, *What We Talk About When We Talk About Love*, his next book, contained stories of longer duration, sentences of less clipped cadences. Some stories in that book were edited and revised so that they *seemed* superficially more like earlier stories. But I'd already seen them in manuscript, and I knew them in the original. Gordon Lish *may* have had a hand in those changes, but they were finally Ray's responsibility. But by the time Ray's third book of stories [Cathedral] had been published, not only was Gordon out of the picture as editor, but the kind of normal changes that go on in any writer's style as one gets older, and learns more, and uses things up, and the demands on one's sentences become different and perhaps greater, these changes were evident. The style and cadence of Ray's sentences had changed. He could still write *short* short stories, but he could do more too. And would've done a great deal more.

People who love Ray's stories sometimes remember them as

seeming more alike than they really are; as in all things love often prospers through the agency of a kind of restrictiveness. But Ray was a more various writer than many of his fans give him credit for. His sympathies enlarged. As he became in his life more comfortable and had a more ample life, his stories became more ample.

As you say, the stories did become longer, more complex, and take on deeper meaning. However, at the risk of oversimplification, they were still about these guys trying to deal with the stuff of their lives; their money problems, their drinking, their women. Then in his last story ["Errand"], about the death of Chekhov, we are suddenly no longer in what one might call Carver country. We are strangely somewhere else. What's your sense of that change?

It would have seemed perfectly normal had Ray lived and written another collection of stories. Change, particularly to change by virtue of broadening one's reach, is something all writers know they must do and should do. But you can't just do it by personal fiat. You have to be at the right place at the right time; you have to be submissive to the change, you must have a changing subject matter which you can make your own. Like all good things for writers, much is fortuitous. And I think that in Ray's writing that story ["Errand"], lightning struck. It was a sign of things to come. Not that he was going to write a series of stories on literary subjects; but he was feeling in that story a kind of exhilaration, a freedom which would've resulted in wonderful work.

Exhilaration?

Ray had a passion and reverence for literature, and particularly for Chekhov. I think he grafted himself onto that piece of Chekhov biography in the same way he had grafted himself onto the bits of life that he knew personally. He just made that be his own.

It wasn't just Chekhov.

No, but it wouldn't be a story if it weren't Chekhov. If the guy dying in bed of TB were someone else, it would be something different. I can't even remember the title most of the time. I always think of it as the Chekhov story.

Or the story of the waiter.

Ray's stories are often about third parties, people looking out windows, glimpsing what seems to be real life in progress.

In this case, while the rest of the world and the reader are concerned with Chekhov dying in his bed, Ray's eye is on the poor waiter staring at the champagne cork on the floor. (Short break)

Everyone I've contacted in preparing this book spoke fondly, even lovingly of Ray. What was the quality that made him so likable?

When Ray was around there was such a sense of mirth and good humor in the air. Something I don't think I'll ever replace. He was a man able to know the worst about you and find good in you irrespective. The parts that were indelibly good (if you had any), he would absorb and respond to. If he liked you, he liked you. If you got off track, he'd find a way to bring you back to his affection. He was a good man to tell your stories to.

How was he on jokes?

It was an odd thing about Ray. He didn't particularly like jokes, and I do like jokes. I told Ray a lot of jokes until I just figured out that he wouldn't respond. It was as though the factitiousness of jokes couldn't compete with the factual humor of life. Even though Ray was an artist and cared very much about making things, his toehold was in real life. Certainly in a lot of Ray's stories, not in all of them, but many, there was a very pronounced sense – it's part of their illusion – that this is about as close as language can come to representing actuality.

Is that what prompted you to say to him that you had read his story about Maryann?

That remark simply indicated how actual the story seemed. I didn't entirely mean to suggest that I thought that was the case, but that the story seemed so actual.

Well, it was.

What do you mean it was?

I mean that the sentiments that he expressed in the story were feasibly close to those he had in his mind about his relationship with Maryann.

Maybe, maybe not. Anyway, it doesn't matter much.

Well, stories just don't come out of thin air.

But in a way they do come out of thin air. If you read a story of mine, or anybody else's, and you ask if I ever knew anybody like this, the answer may be absolutely no. Or did you ever hear anybody say this line. The answer may be absolutely no, I made it up. Fiction is made up.

Certainly. But why is your fiction your fiction, and Ray's fiction his fiction, and Lenny Michaels's fiction his? Every writer has his story to tell that comes from his experience.

There's a line from Henry James that says experience is sensibility. That's a remark which hopes to blur the relation between fiction and precedent event.

And sensibility comes from what you have lived through. Look, I'm sorry, I don't want this to appear like an argument. I'll cut it out.

No, leave it in. Stories are basically made up of language, not of events. They aren't made of things you've done. They may sometimes seem to refer to things you've done.

Or seen.

Or seen, but committed to language. They can just as often though be language that represents absolutely nothing you've *ever* done or seen or thought about.

I believe that, Richard. I also believe you write the way you do because of everything that has happened to you in your life.

But that's a truism.

Well then, it's true. I'm glad you didn't say that it was sheer bullshit.

(Laughs) It's not bullshit. It's bullshit's sneaky cousin, a truism.

(Laughs) *Ray's stories were based on his experience –*
(Emphatically) I don't concede that. I don't concede that
because you weren't there, and neither was I.

No, I wasn't. But these interviews demonstrate that you
have your perspective on Ray, and Toby Wolff has his,
which is similar but still different from Geoffrey's, and
Tess Gallagher has hers, and Bill Kittredge has still
another. Everyone I interviewed sees Ray through his or
her own periscope. But what seems to emerge from all
this is that Ray was able to – and here I don't believe I'm
diminishing his art –
You may be, actually by shifting attention away from it.

No, I don't believe I am. Again, I'm going to have to cut
some of this out.
No, leave it in.

What I'm trying to say is that all one has to do is try
to do what Ray did, and they'll soon discover how
impossible it is. Ray's power was in the way he could
examine his experience and create art based on it.
That just isn't a formula that I have any respect for.

I don't see it as a formula.
Well, it's formulaic: You have a life. You make art out of
life. That leaves out too much, too much that goes into making
stories.

But when you say make art out of life – God! To make
art out of anything is such a difficult task. To make art
out of life, there's the challenge, it seems to me. I'm not
talking about case histories.
I just don't like the notion of Ray making art out of life
because, in that way of expressing it, he's responsible to life,
more than he's responsible to art. I've always supposed that
Ray, as a writer, was responsible principally to the integrity of
his stories. This, even though he *may* have believed the most
memorable, ringing things that lived in his life were not stories
but lived life. At any point in the writing of "Intimacy," I believe his fidelity is to the best next line he can write. That line

may have some vagrant origin in experience transmuted by memory and the demands of writing sentences, but it may be absolutely out of no experience. It may be something whose origin he has no idea of, except it comes in his mind – like a little lightning bug. And as long as that's true, and I know that it *is* true, I would say stories are best thought of as being made up and not wedded to life, except of course after they're made and the reader takes them back to his or her life.

I recognize that. What I mean is – the word that comes to mind is the word impulse. For instance, the impulse to write "Intimacy." Of course he didn't have to actually visit Maryann to write that story. He visited her in his mind. He's at his keyboard, alone in his room writing a story. And he's saying, I am visiting her – I say to her such and such – the whole story is a monologue of a narrator's remembered conversation with his ex-wife.
I simply disagree with all of that.

I trust you don't believe I am denigrating Ray's achievement.

No, but I prefer sticking up for the primacy of imagination, rather than the importance of prior experience. OK, sure, Ruskin wrote, "You cannot have a landscape by Turner without having a country for him to paint." But I'm just interested in the painting. And as for writers, all I know is that we write one line, then another line, then another.

I don't believe I diminish a writer's creativity when I admire his gift to make art out of his life experience. Look, if all there was to writing a story was in the telling, you could go down to the corner filling station and sooner or later someone will tell a story that will knock your socks off. Writing the story, though, is an entirely different matter. Ray was able to write stories that evoked in us the same emotional response, as though the story had been told directly to us by someone we cared about.

Maybe. I would certainly have to have him *tell* me the

story in order to answer that. I try to isolate my responses to a story to the facts of them. I like them better that way.

Then I must go back to ask if he created his stories out of thin air?

By which you mean if he writes about a bankrupt, was he ever a bankrupt? My guess is that a lot of things Ray did in one way or another provoked the stories. But beyond saying that, I don't know any more. Only he knew, and I don't care; because to me all that matters is that I read the story. I don't care if Ray had those specific experiences. I just happen to know that once you've committed something to language, experience of any kind, language alters it. There was a trick that Robert Lowell used to play (it's in the Hamilton biography) when trying to perfect a line in a poem and he couldn't get it right. One of the things he did was put the word "not" in front of the verb, which reversed the meaning of the sentence. But it also added a beat to the line. I think Ray cared more about adding a beat to the line than representing actually, or adequately, or even tangentially or remotely what actually happened. Ray was an artist when he sat down to write. If it meant tampering with actuality, lying about it, perverting or distorting it, saying x was y, and y was x, he'd do it to make a better story. Consequently to my mind, tracing things back to life is idle. It's to me gossip of a not very informative kind, even of a misleading kind. *(Short break)*

Some critics who say Ray kept writing the story of his life –

That's one more arrogant disservice to his work. There are many others more pernicious than that. I don't find much interest in psychologizing writers. I don't like to be psychologized myself.

I don't suppose it's some critics' function to be mindful.

No. Just to be fair and smart. *(Laughs)*

Then what does the word minimalism in regard to Ray's work summon up for you?

Nothing at all.

Geoffrey Wolff's answer to that question was "bullshit."
He *would* say it better than I do. *(Laughs)*

*All the others I interviewed had their own little tale to
tell about Ray. They're often funny but somehow always
show that endearing quality of his that all remember
and miss so much.*

Well, I remember at SMU the day after I had met Ray I
knew I'd met a guy I liked. On the morning after I had met
him, I was in my hotel room asleep actually, and the phone
rang. Ray was on the phone. It was the first call I ever got
from Ray, and he seemed jittery. He said, "Richard, would you
mind coming over to my room?" I asked why. He said, "There's
a woman downstairs in the lobby, and she's coming up to my
room and I don't want to be alone here with her." I thought
that was very funny and agreed to come over. And so here
were two guys sitting on the bed, shooting the breeze, when
this woman came up. I didn't know who she was. I was the sort
of duenna for that little meeting. After an uncomfortable period of time, much to Ray's relief, the woman left. I guess that
was a nice entree to Ray's life, though I never knew what had
gone on with the two of them. He was a kind of rascal in a way.
He was always trying to cope in the present with his occasionally rash acts in the past. That's natural in all human beings,
but it was particularly vivid with Ray.

*That story seems so characteristic of Ray. Bill
Kittredge tells how shortly after meeting him, Ray
was up in Montana for a visit; Chuck Kinder tells of
Ray knocking on his door the day after meeting him;
and you getting this phone call the day after meeting
him. Everyone speaks of his genuine shyness, but I
suppose once he considered you as his friend, he could
drop his guard.*

Ray had no difficulty making friends, and he valued
friends a lot, though if you ever betrayed him, as a few people
did in his life, he held it against you fiercely and forever. I think
back in the days when he met Bill and Chuck; he was drinking,
and he was on the run from a difficult domestic situation, so it's
not surprising that he'd seek solace with his friends. Espe-

cially when you consider they were writers he admired and about the same age. One of the things that drew Ray to people was a sense of mutuality: unspeakable things you have done and wanted to be forgiven for; recognizing opportunities you'd seized to be generous; or wanting to do one thing excellently. Once you could hook up with Ray along those lines, then you had a connection with him that was very solid. As Ray got older, his life became so full, people wanting to do things for him, wanting him to do things in the world, he became less and less likely to show up at your door.

Jay McInerney remarked to me that Ray, in his modesty, never appreciated the effect he had on younger writers. When Jay edited the Random Review, *he read hundreds of manuscripts, and he perceived nearly all of them as being versions and derivative of Carver stories. Did you see that effect?*

Myself, I don't think it's true that nearly all writers younger than Ray were influenced by him; and I can say that with perfect ease, because my work *was* affected by him, and I think healthily so, I'm glad to say. But Ray never spoke to me in those terms. That may have been due to his modesty – which was genuine – but it also had to do with something Ray knew and cherished. It was that short stories are received forms. Ray didn't write the first one, and neither did Hemingway, nor did Sherwood Anderson or Chekhov. Insofar as it is a form that Ray and I and Jay inherit, it's natural and inevitable that certain influences occur. There's a mentality, particularly among book reviewers in America, which when it finds evidence of influence in the work of a writer wants to create a ranking, which purports that the work which demonstrates influence is less worthy than the prior work. Some spurious sense of purity. I don't think Ray believed that. He believed that influence was natural, that you learn to write stories from other people, from their work; that one of the reasons he seemed unaware of his influence was that it was so native to him.

Native to him?

The fact that influence existed. That he was influenced,

and that he might influence other writers. He knew he was influenced by John Gardner and writers he admired, John Cheever and Hemingway and Chekhov. He didn't think it was a big deal. He knew many people read his stories and that that would willy-nilly create an influence. All that mattered was that the influence have a good effect, that it might somehow influence some writer to write a good story better. Assessing influence is a lame way to appraise art, although it's easy. I prefer to try to appraise art in absolute terms, and Ray's work was absolutely excellent.

We haven't spoken about his poetry. Some have said that he'd rather write poems than stories.

The last couple of years of his life he was intent on writing poems. This is just my opinion, but I think it was easier for him to write poems.

Easier to express himself in poetry?
Or the actual process?

I think he found poetry more pleasurable because it was less vexatious. I mean, Ray was not a man who enjoyed hard work. *(Laughs)*

Few of us do.

(Still laughing) Few of us do, right. I remember when Ray came up to visit and Kristina and I were living in Vermont, this was in 1978. We were living in a big refurbished barn owned by a descendant of James McNeill Whistler, and it was quite nice. Ray allowed how nice it was to live out in the woods with wonderful views and wood fires every night, coziness and the whole nine yards. One morning I hooked the trailer to the tractor and, needing a little help, I asked Ray to come with me. He said OK, OK. He got on the trailer and after we started down the road he said to me, "Wait a minute. Where are we going?" I said we were going off to cut wood. He said, "Do what?" I repeated, "Cut wood." And he said, "Maybe I'd better go back to the house." *(Laughs)* He didn't like to do any kind of work. I think there were a few occasions when he wished that he did, but his heart was never in it. He'd never walk when he could ride.

What about his interest in poetry?

It's clear to me that Ray loved poetry. He and Tess and I would fetch up together, particularly after they'd established their lives in Port Angeles. We'd sit around at night in Tess's house and read poems aloud to each other. Ray read to me the first time I ever heard it, Richard Hugo's poem, "Degrees of Gray in Phillipsburg." Poetry was very fundamental to what his understanding of literary art was. But I have to think it was something he could do with ease, which isn't to say he cared about it less. He did it because it was easier for him than cranking up the machinery for a short story. Ray could sit around the house of a morning, smoke cigarettes, look out the window, and write a couple of poems that pleased him.

He said that at times he had written ten or twelve poems in a month.

Oh, he did. But when he wrote short stories, he'd start by getting the whole thing out in one bout of writing. He'd try to stay at that story, unstopping until he finished it, starting early in the morning until late at night, trying to get the whole thing out in one continuous utterance.

That could be wearing.

He could do that for a while, but then he needed relief. Ray certainly could have written novels if he'd ever wanted to. There was nothing in him that stopped him from writing novels. I know he was committed to writing a novel when he died, but it wouldn't have surprised me if the very laborious nature of writing a novel wouldn't finally have discouraged him a bit.

Didn't he say in interviews that he was working on a novel?

He may well have been.

Perhaps something may turn up someday.

I certainly have every confidence he could have written a wonderful novel, but I don't think he wanted to that much.

Do you believe that bothered him at all?

Not a bit. You know, there's another spurious dictum of literary life which says that if you write short stories that's fine, but you're not really a writer until you write novels. That's ridiculous. Ray was a wonderful writer writing his stories and poems. He didn't need to write a novel to prove anything. If he wanted to, he would have written it wonderfully.

We were talking about Ethan Canin earlier. He told me he was working on a novel because everyone is after him to write one. It is expected of him.

That's probably the economics of publishing. Novels are supposedly easier to sell to readers than short stories. That may be a prophecy that publishers fulfill themselves.

A Raymond Carver novel would have built-in big sales.

Sure. Cheever wrote *The Wapshot Scandal* and *Bullet Park* supposedly because of publishing pressures.

You are a switch hitter, known for your novels as well as your collection of short stories. They're both hard work. Do you favor one over the other?

No. I don't like qualitative differences over literary forms. If I could write a beautiful sestina, believe me I would.

I'm glad you said that. Some poets might take umbrage with your earlier statement about short stories being more difficult to write than poetry.

Poets are frequently in the business of taking umbrage. *(Laughs)* I didn't say poetry was easier. I said it came easier for Ray. It certainly doesn't come easy for me.

I've never seen a poem of yours.

Well, you may not live that long, Sam. *(Laughs)*

Getting back to safer ground, would you tell me what you think about the titles of Ray's stories?

I always liked his titles, particularly *Will You Please Be Quiet, Please?* They often seemed arbitrary and hooked onto the story; but as titles they seem to be quirky, and affecting, and new. Sometimes it's true; somebody will mention the title of a story, and I won't know which the hell story it is. I was never a student of Ray's work, though. I've read all the stories maybe only twice in my life. Ray wasn't a great literary figure to me – he was my pal.

*Did your pal ever give you a clue as to how he went
about choosing those great titles?*

I never knew if he was the guy who always dreamed up
the titles. I know in the early stories Gordon Lish had a big
influence on Ray, in large measure a good influence, and maybe
Gordon helped him with a title. But no matter where the title
comes from, if you read it on the side of a bus, or your wife suggests it to you, if you stick it on your story, it's your title. I'll
never know why he changed the title of one of my most favorite stories, "What Is It?" to "Are These Actual Miles?"

Why didn't you like that title?

Because it gives away the story's best line. Ray was a
guy who, although he was very reluctant to take any literary
suggestions from me, would listen if he thought the person had
his best interest at heart, was very smart, and had good literary judgment. Maybe I fell outside of the box on all of those.

Who were these people he'd listen to?

He would listen to his editors; Chip McGrath at the *New
Yorker* for one, a man he admired very much. He certainly lis-
tened to Tess. Finally, though, it doesn't make much difference
how the stories came into being what they were, because they
were his and only his.

*What was his general reaction to his editors'
suggestions?*

I really don't know. I think finally he felt he could bounce
things off of Tess, and Tess was smart about stories. He felt he
had as much help as he needed. It should be said that he published stories in magazines, and they got edited there.

Leonard Michaels

*Could you say something about the misunderstanding
you once had with Ray?*

I wrote a letter asking him to write an essay for a book
I was doing. In the letter I reminded him of one of the parties and made a big joke out of it. I have a feeling that letter

irritated him. He didn't want to be reminded. He didn't want to be reminded in the way that I reminded him. I think that was it. I'm not sure. I was very lighthearted and laughing when I wrote the letter, and I thought he'd get a big kick out of it, but he never made any reference to it. So I decided it was a stupid letter, the wrong thing to do. I didn't fully understand what was going on in his life. Naturally we never mentioned that letter. I still have it and look at it every now and then, and regret it.

Did you ever get the essay?

No. He was completely and legally bound to the *New Yorker* at that point. He couldn't do anything without offering it to them first. He seemed to be very happy to have this contract. It represented some kind of . . . *(pause, searching for word)*

Security?

I don't think it was security but more like acknowledgment that he had arrived. Like getting a diploma maybe. He marveled at the amount of money they gave him for signing the contract, seven thousand dollars. He said the number as if it were a thing. A miracle number-thing that had dropped into his life. I suppose, after all he had been through, any good thing still surprised him, so he spoke in a tone that suggested he couldn't understand how this was happening to an ordinary, unlucky guy like himself. He wasn't all that awed. He may have intended to sound that way only to hold off the demonic forces, the ones that are sure to punish you if you take any pleasure in anything in your life.

I remember seeing Ray greet you so warmly, embracing you, in Port Townsend one day in August '87. What was that all about?

I hadn't seen Ray for a very long time. There had been that one bit of communication – that letter – which was a mistake, as I've said. He came by to visit me in Port Townsend from his house in Port Angeles, and I was very glad that he had, because in a way, to tell you the truth, I felt forgiven for having written that stupid letter. I was very glad to see him, glad when he stepped out of his – was it a Mercedes? You were there –

Yes, a Mercedes.

When we first met, he owned a VW bug. It was always strewn with unpaid traffic tickets and emergency room receipts and other such evidence of the high-stress little miseries of his daily life. His Mercedes was clean. His big hug told me we were friends, there was no ill feeling. But there was one other reason that I suspected there might be some negative element in our friendship. It had to do with the fact that I was once asked to judge a writing contest. I had this huge pile of manuscripts, and I was going crazy trying to do the job, trying to read through this pile of stuff. And Ray called up in the middle of it and said, I hear you're judging this so and so writing contest, and I said yes. And he said, Well, you know so-and-so has submitted a manuscript. And I said, Yes it's true, I've seen his name. And Ray said, Well, he's really a very good writer and blah, blah. Anyhow that made it impossible for me to give this guy the prize. I don't know that I would have, but I do know I might have. And after Ray's phone call I was so totally fucked up that all I could think of was now if I give this guy the prize, I'll never know if I'd acted in an honest way. So I ended up not doing it and feeling compromised. That was a negative thing. Years went by and what can I say, aaagh, it was awful. And then the next thing was this letter. Maybe my stupid letter was a bit hostile. It may have been a hostile letter, though I thought it was hilariously funny. He didn't think so one bit. So that's why this meeting in Port Townsend was a very important occasion, because as I said, it meant I was forgiven, and I wanted that. And then he talked to me about how well he had been doing. There was this evidence of his car, and he told me he had two sailboats, and how well he'd been doing in Europe as well as in the United States, and that the money was coming in and coming in. I had a feeling he was saying that my faith in him had been justified. I was very happy for him. He looked great – Eddie Bauer country gentleman outfit. Remember? His relation to money was a little complicated. He had doubts about enjoying it. He said, I got this boat and I go out and sit in it and I'm thinking why the hell am I out on this boat. I should be home writing. *(Laughs)* Then there were a couple of other things. Apparently now that he had money, certain people were hitting on him. That bothered him.

He wrote about that in "Elephant." I felt so good watching you two guys hugging and laughing it up there. Of course, I didn't know all that was going on then.

Well, that's what we talked about. I could see quite clearly enough that he was enjoying himself enormously. He was enjoying life in many ways. He looked very, very good. He had this big car, and he told me about his boats. He was triumphant and his French editor was right there walking around, admiring Ray every minute. All in all it amounted to a kind of relief for me. I could now with a clear mind and heart pick up the phone and call him any time and talk with him. Not that I hadn't been able to earlier, but there were those little stupid things. I felt happy for him. I'd never stopped loving him. As it happened, some time after that, not too long, I did pick up the phone and call him and heard the horrible news. It wasn't too long after that, was it?

No, not too long – about two months later.

I could hardly talk when he told me what had happened. I choked up although he was quite sanguine about the whole thing. An operation had been performed. His surgeon told Ray he had read his stories. He loved them. Ray said that there was nothing to worry about, he was all better, out of the woods.

Richard Ford

Did you ever see Ray and Maryann together?

Not while Ray was alive. I saw them together when Ray was dead.

That's when I first met you, in Montana. You had just come from Ray's funeral. Could you say anything about that?

Well, having been to a lot of funerals in my life, I didn't

find it to be much out of the ordinary. Out of the ordinary maybe only in one sense – that Tess not only allowed but invited Maryann and Chris and some of Maryann's immediate family to the funeral. Tess was just trying to say that this is your ex-husband and this is your father, and we all loved him, and now he's gone, and we have to bury him, and I don't want to exclude you. It was very generous of her. Other than that, no, there wasn't anything unusual.

Was there much drinking?
At the funeral? I don't remember. But there was food. It was all in the American tradition in which the neighbors bring pies. It's a little like Christmas, except somebody's dead. Other than that, how people express their grief, and the stresses that grief places on people – particularly in familial situations such as Ray's was – all that is private.

Well, everyone there loved him deeply and was under
heavy emotional strain, and it was a great shock –
It wasn't a great surprise. We knew he was dying.

When I say shock, I mean although they expected him to
die, there was always the hope that perhaps he'd recover,
but what they had to deal with now was the reality –
Well, as I said, Ray kept the most grievous things to himself if he could. The last month of his life, perhaps the last two months of his life, he pretty much packed it in. He kept to himself and Tess. The goings and comings of his day-to-day life were pretty much just the two of them together. He worked hard, we now know. I talked to him fairly often during that period, not as often as usual. I remember he called me up one day and told me that his son, Vance, was there. Vance had come in from Germany. Ray sounded quite agitated. His kids agitated him. He loved them, but they agitated him. He said, "Look, I'm going to put Vance on the phone. Would you talk to Vance?" I said, "Sure, I'll talk to Vance." And I talked to Vance about what – I don't even remember. We just talked. I've known Vance since he was a teenager, and I like him very much. I think Ray just wanted Vance to know, in some very indirect

way, that he had a friend in me. I only talked to Ray a couple of times after that. It must have been mid-June 1988.

During this period of time, Ray was telling all the reporters and writers that he had this thing licked, that he was coming out of it. And of course he hadn't. What was he telling you?

Nothing explicit. I think it was a tenet of our friendship that I wouldn't ask him if there weren't some special reason, and there wasn't. I knew he'd had a recurrence in the winter before, in February, and I knew he'd had another recurrence. It was typical of me, and typical of our friendship, that I wasn't keeping tabs on him. I wasn't calling him up and taking his pulse all the time, because I wanted to try, and he wanted to try, to keep normal life going.

It wasn't exactly denial, but nevertheless you didn't want to –

No, I'm not a denier of things like that, and he wasn't in a position to deny anything. The last time I laid eyes on him, he looked like hell, I know that. He was very puffy and bloated. There was no denial. He had just so many days left to live and wanted to get the most out of them, not succumb to gloominess.

Where was that?

At the American Booksellers Association in June at Anaheim. We gave a reading together. It was the last reading he ever gave. He was going on with things.

And at that time he was telling people he was recovering.

He seemed troubled to me. I remember saying to him, "Look, Curley," I used to call him Curley. I said, "You seem fine to me, you look fine. This is all going to work out right." And he looked at me and said in a very grave voice, "Well, I hope so," which was the least hopeful words I'd ever heard him say.

You were his friend. At the same time, he was telling others that he had this thing licked.

He had not long come back from the doctors at that

time, and he'd been told that he was dying, that he wouldn't live very long. This was maybe three weeks before he and Tess got married. I don't know what he was telling the world about his illness. He did not tell me, though, that he'd been given the black spot.

What was your reaction to their marriage?

I tend to be kind of blithe about people's decisions to get married. But there was much more poignance to the situation than was apparent to me at the time. I was in Salt Lake City, and I was supposed to fly over to Reno to be their witness, but I couldn't. The timing was just impossible.

Do you regret not going?

No, it's much better that I didn't go. I would have loved to have done that with them, but really that was something that they were happiest to do alone. They would have included me, if it could have worked out, but given the fact that it was so near to his death, it was far better that they did that by themselves. They were very close.

What was your reaction to the first news of his illness?

Earlier in the summer of '87, Kristina and I and Tess and Ray had been to England and France together. We had a very good time, but I noticed Ray looked thin and kind of gaunt. He seemed from time to time to be not completely well. I had a sense that something was amiss with him. Ray was never a healthy-seeming man. He ate horrible things, smoked a million cigarettes, he'd been through the ravages of liquor. He'd given his body a lot of big whacks. Sometimes I'd go over to his house and he'd go to the store and come back with a sack of doughnuts and Twinkies and God knows what else. I'd laugh and say, "Ray, I hate to see you bring that stuff in here," and he'd say, "You'll feel different about it at twelve o'clock to-night." And he was right.

He seemed to have a thing about doughnuts.

Sweets, cakes, that kind of stuff. But, anyway, we used to talk on the phone a couple times a week, and sometime in August of '87, over a series of phone calls in which I'd talk to Tess and then to Ray, it was divulged that he'd had a bad chest X-ray, and he'd probably need surgery. It was all done in a hush-hush manner, because he was distressed by it, and Ray hated bad news. He'd had enough in his lifetime. All through September he had all kinds of tests, and it was never ascertained that he had lung cancer until he had the surgery.

Could you tell us something about his attitude then?

I remember I was in Boston on a book tour the weekend before he was going in for exploratory lung surgery. I flew over to Syracuse to spend Sunday with him, because he was antsy as hell about the operation, and nervous and afraid. Naturally, Toby was there, and of course Tess. I never will forget that when he took me out to the airport when I left, we talked at great length about how he was going to get through it. And once he penetrated the necessary nervousness, he seemed resolved. Ray was a real grown-up. That line in his story where he says, "I've seen some things." Well, he'd seen some things all right, and he knew he was going to see some more. It didn't surprise him. He just hated it. Hated it in a way that you can hate bad news and then finally surrender to it and muscle up. Which is what he did.

His fears were tragically well founded. Did he ever tell you that he did not expect to have a long life?

Oh yes. Part of his view of the world was get it now, seize it now, because we're not going to be around a long time. He didn't mean it in a morbid way, just in a realistic way. He often said he'd died once and came back to life, referring to his drinking, and he felt that the second life was not going to be a long one. I never thought he'd live long. He didn't conduct himself like a man who was planning on a long life. Just a good one.

In his beautiful essay "Friendship," Ray wrote about how he treasured the bond of friendship he shared with you and Toby Wolff. However, he goes on to say in the essay that it doesn't follow that he would give up his place in the lifeboat for you. He may not have expected a long life, but in this essay, at least, it doesn't seem that he was eager to go. The only

*alternative to burying your friends, he said, was to
have them bury you.*

Yes, I think he would rather have buried me than have me
bury him. He wanted to live.

*Others have described the ingenuous pleasure he took in
his boat, his house, his Mercedes after the deprivations
of his so-called previous life. What is your recollection
of this?*

Oh, he wouldn't hesitate to call you up to tell you about
his latest good fortune. But he always made it clear that he
wanted to share it with you. It was never bragging. The way I
and most of his friends felt was that it was ratifying. It meant
that a man as earnest, and unguileful, and as hard working and
accessible as Ray could make something which the world
deemed excellent. It made me feel that it was worthwhile to
keep on with what I was doing. I'm sure his other friends felt
the same way.

*I like your word, ratifying. You've portrayed Ray in a
fine light.*

Ray was never a writer standing off from me. He was
very close to me, so I can't stand back from him. Nor do I want
to. My memories of him are very personal. One of the reasons I
suppose I haven't written anything about him is that I don't
want my memories of him to become fixed, unreflecting. I
want them to stay fluid and supple – full as they always were.

Stephen Dobyns

*What did you think of his later stories such as
"Blackbird Pie" and "Errand"?*

What he had discovered by then was a kind of confidence.
He knew if he got an idea for a story he could turn it into a
good one. He was very convinced of what the good reviewers
said of him. When he received good reviews, he'd send
copies to his friends. Tess strengthened him and helped him
gain assurance, but he also gloried in these reviews. He also

depended hugely on his friends – Toby Wolff, Geoffrey Wolff, Richard Ford, Michael Ryan. We'd praise his work, he'd listen very carefully, and he grew from it.

We've heard much about his Bad Raymond days. How did he seem to you after he sobered up?

Alcoholics, when they turn sober, may be sober but they still maintain many of their old eccentricities. Ray really changed. The only thing that remained the same for me was that when he'd pick up the phone there was still the old paranoid hushed voice cautiously checking who was calling.

I remember he was giving a benefit reading for *Ploughshares* in Boston, where I was living. At that time he was being followed around by a *Life* magazine photographer. They were doing a story on Ray. I was struck by how far he had come from his fragile condition when I had first met him in '78. By this time in '84 or '85 he had a fine sense of himself as a writer, such confidence in himself. He was an entirely different person at that point. At the reception for him after the reading, Ray had very little interest in the photographer, who was climbing all over him taking shots. The guy must have shot at least eight rolls of film. I was impressed with the way Ray handled himself through all this – the kind of belief and simple pride he had in himself without any signs of hubris. He was truly a person at that point with confidence in his abilities and looking forward with hope to what he would accomplish. He had changed entirely from the nervous, anxious person I had known in '78, and he was distinguished in a way that touched me. Yet that childlike quality of his that made him so wonderful to be with never left him. I don't know, if they could choose who should stay and who should die, they certainly took one of the sweetest ones away when they took him.

Where were you when you heard that he had died?

At a writers' conference in Maine. I heard on the radio that he had died. There was no way I could go to the funeral. I talked to Richard Ford afterward and to Tess and Doug Unger. It sounded kind of hellish with the tension between Maryann and Tess there. Maryann was very upset. Ray did not want to be embalmed. His prejudices – he didn't want that fluid in him. Ford said it was an open casket. He said – I've never forgotten his phrase – that Ray was green as a pickle.

Chris Carver

You were at the burial service –
The funeral itself consisted of family and friends. I met my dad's close writer friends. I mainly recall his editor, Gary Fisketjon, Richard Ford and his wife, Kristina, and my dad's agent, Amanda Urban. Family members said pieces and remembrances. A beautiful piece by Doug Unger and another by my mother. Tess read poems from his last collection, *A New Path to the Waterfall*. I read "The Car" from *Ultramarine*, which drew smiles from an otherwise somber crowd. It was my daughter Windy's favorite of her grandfather's work. Ironically, my old Chevy Monza had blown a rod the day before. I asked that everyone join hands at the end of the service for the Lord's Prayer as they do at the end of AA meetings, in respect and gratitude for my dad's sobriety.

It was hard. Hard seeing his casket lowered into the ground. We had a visit planned that first week in August when my summer session classes at college were over.

Is there anything more you wish to say?
I suppose there could literally be a book written on what has taken place since my dad's death. Things were brought up to me at the funeral about my dad's will and about my inheritance that I was emotionally unable to deal with at the time. I was under extreme stress, eight and a half months pregnant, and didn't want to be dealing with such matters at a time like that. However, one thing is clear. There was an irrevocable father-daughter bond between us. On one of our "hotel" visits in 1986, while sitting in a lounge waiting for our Chinese takeout, my dad's eyes welled up as he said to me, "Nobody knows, do they? Nobody knows." *(Pause)*

He revisited his past so much in his writing because it had

so much emotional impact on him. I would not have wanted any man in the world to be my father but Raymond Carver.

Geoffrey Wolff

Ray wrote frequently, especially in his poems, about death. Did he ever speak to you about death?

No, no, and I mean no. We had one discussion once and it had nothing to do with literature. It was after I'd had a heart operation, and it was shortly before Ray found out that he was sick. I had written something about this operation and the events leading up to it. And very characteristic of me, the seriousness in that piece came from what I hoped was a comic imagination. I don't believe I can be accused of solemnity. So Ray had taken some pleasure from the piece, but when I spoke to him about the origin of the piece and explained some of the details of the illness, it was the only time I ever noticed him uneasy around me. He did not want to talk about bad luck or bad news. The subject of illness or death was not at all welcome. On the page, it was a different matter, but not face to face.

I'm sure you spoke to him after he discovered he had cancer. What was the scope of those conversations?

I had several conversations with him after he found out. He was going to have an operation at one point that was similar to one I'd had, and I wanted to tell him as much as he wanted to know about that particular operation. He asked me some questions about it, but he told me going in exactly what he did not want to know about it. I know I'd want to know all I could; after all, knowledge is power. But not Ray. He wanted, as he said, to wake up three months later and find out it was all fixed, that it was all over.

Would you call it denial?

No, although I think Ray was perfectly capable of denial. I'd say it was more that Ray believed in the power of language so profoundly, it was so sacred to him, that he understood, as few people understand, that words are loaded pistols. Sometimes to say something, to name it, is to enact it. So there were certain words he would not say.

Did you attend the funeral service, the wake for Ray in Port Angeles?

No, I was out of the country at the time, but I heard about it.

What did you hear about it?

Oh, that emotions were running very high. I believe the thing I would like to say about what I heard was that the way I understand Ray was laid out for viewing was a scene that only Ray himself could have done justice to in a story. A story that would have been peculiarly Carverlike in its plangency, sadness, and high comedy. The scene of the open display of the body was something that he as a great writer could have appreciated. That's about as much as I care to get into here.

OK – Ray wrote so many, but which of his stories did you personally favor, and perhaps tell us why?

Well, I do have a couple, and they come from different periods. We were talking before about "Why Don't You Dance?" What I admire most about that story is again the extraordinary speed in which you perceive the lives of the young, callow couple. Then you see her deepen right in front of you. At the end of the story, there are two lightning-fast changes of direction. At the very end, when she calls him the poor old guy, or something like that, and she tells the story of this old guy with all his furniture out there in his front yard. Then her mood darkens and she realizes it's her life too, the culmination of her life, that we're all in the same boat. I like that story.

The story "What We Talk About When We Talk About Love" I admire so much because first of all I don't think there has ever been anything even approximately as good written about drinking. I've done enough drinking in my life to know how it feels, what happens to syntax, what happens to diction, as the light begins to come down in the room, and the stuff goes further down in the bottle. The room darkens, and you see your whole life darken too. The only other writer who can do that kind of story is Cheever. Cheever stories do have that kind of quality.

But the two stories that absolutely knock me off my pins are "Cathedral," which surprised me – that story takes a turn I never anticipated, although I knew Ray's heart was capacious enough to have written a story like that. It was a daring story, perhaps the most touching story, for me, that he had written. I think it shows extraordinary skill – Ray always had skill – but this story has an emotional precision, a predictable willingness to surrender to strangeness. The whole situation is so strange. But, brilliantly, the emotional relationship between the narrator and the blind man becomes so direct and so *uneccentric* (which may be the word I'm looking for) and so credibly human. It's us at our best, people at their best.

Then there's the story that if it didn't teach me something about writing there's something wrong with me, and that's "Errand." I remember reading it in the *New Yorker*, reading about the death of Chekhov, and I'm a biographer as well as a novelist, and it starts out, as you know, as a conventional biography about the last days of a great man. I thought I understood what was happening, and I was puzzled by it. It took a bit of patience, because I was finding it almost tedious at the beginning. I didn't know where he was going with this story. Then after Chekhov has died, and the waiter comes on, all disheveled, waiting for his tip, and spots the champagne cork lying on the rug, and steps on it so they won't notice it, I realized then where Ray's eye had been all during that story. His eye had been on the guy no one ever notices, standing offstage, and he's the most important character in the story. I was deeply affected by that. I realized how many of us have had our eyes on the wrong characters. Ray had something to teach us, and he did.

> *It's curious that you should focus on that aspect of Ray's writing. When I asked your brother Toby for a characteristic example of Ray's writing, he chose the poem "The Baker," the one about Pancho Villa and Count Vronsky taking over this Mexican baker's house and wife and waving pistols around. The poem ends*

with this little baker sneaking off barefoot, in fear of his
life. Ray writes that the baker is the hero of this poem.
All along we've been looking at Vronsky and Villa,
which is just about the same point you make about
"Errand." You brothers are amazing.

You said earlier that everybody seemed to love Ray.
What did you find in him most engaging?

It's probably important to say right here to keep this in
perspective that Ray was a great liar, a wonderful liar. I'll tell
you a story about that. I have a sailboat, and Ray, and Richard
Ford, and my brother Toby and I went out on the boat over to
Block Island. Richard and my brother and I went ashore to do
some drinking. Of course, Ray couldn't be interested in that.
So we left him aboard, and he wanted to know where the coffee
was. I told him the stove was pretty complicated, and it could
easily blow up, and I'd bring him back some coffee because I
didn't want him to use the stove. I gave him my orders on that.
And he said, "Oh Jesus, I wouldn't dream of touching that
stove. I don't truly need the coffee that much anyway." I told
him again if he wanted any, I'd be glad to bring some back for
him. He said, No, he'd be all right. So we left him and went into
town and somehow drifted into a bar. My brother wanted to
talk about literature, and Richard and I wanted to talk about
waitresses, which is what we were looking at there. Pretty
soon we thought it was time to go back to Ray, so we took one
of the waitresses back with us to take our picture, and we got
into the dinghy. When we got close, I noticed Ray was back in
the stern of the boat, as far back as he could get, and he looked
awful. As a matter of fact what he looked like was very dirty.
So I asked him what the hell happened. He said, "Don't worry
about a thing. I've just been shooting smack into my eyeballs."
I knew he was joking, but the waitress was terrified. I knew it
was a joke and went below to get my camera. Now my boat is a
beautiful boat, and below it used to be all white. But now it
was black, soot everywhere. It was completely black. It took
me and my son, Nicholas, ten years to scrape all that damn
soot off. I was so mad. I said, "Jesus, Ray. Son of a bitch, you
shouldn't have done that." He said, "What are you talking
about? I didn't do a damn thing." I said, "Come on, Ray, you lit

that stove. God, Ray, I told you to keep away from it." "I don't know what you're talking about," he said. "I was sleeping for a while. Maybe someone came aboard, but what are you talking about?" I told him to look down below. He said, That's just the way it looked when you guys left. It took us ten years to finally scour that boat down clean. Sometimes, like now, remembering Ray, I wonder if I shouldn't have left it the way it got that morning in the harbor at Block Island, Carvered.

Chuck Kinder

*Did you ever hear Ray say that he expected to
die young?*

Yes, a few times. But it wasn't like a grand, romantic prediction of the artist dying young bullshit variety. I think he really believed it. He really did have a premonition, if you believe in those sorts of things. I remember him talking about it one time in particular. I was the writer in residence at the University of Alabama at Tuscaloosa in the spring of 1980, and I arranged for Ray to give a reading. He and Tess were in Syracuse then. At any rate, the day after the reading we took the Southern Crescent train down to New Orleans, where we joined up with Richard and Kristina Ford for a holiday. Richard had a room reserved for Ray and me in a great little hotel on Toulouse, right off Bourbon Street. We'd all sit out on that balcony at night and sip champagne, except Ray of course, in the hot dark and tell lies. We had a great few days together. One afternoon, Ray and I were knocking around the Quarter when it began to pour rain, so we ducked into this museum off of Jackson Square and started wandering around. We came upon an exhibit of a death mask of Napoleon, and Ray was absolutely fascinated by it. I had to drag him away. Later that night, Ray and I pulled chairs up to the big window that overlooked the courtyards in back, put our feet up, and watched the rain while we passed joints and bullshit back and forth. It was then that he told me for the first time how close he'd come to committing suicide after he quit drinking and thought he'd never be able to write again. He talked about

Tessie a lot that night too. What all she had meant to him staying sober, and how he thought in a lot of ways she had saved his life. He also kept bringing up that death mask of Napoleon, and maybe he should get fitted for one too before long, because of that old feeling that he wouldn't be around long. At that point Ray had about eight more years, I guess.

Did you keep in touch with him all through his illness?

Yes, of course. As a matter of fact, the summer before he became ill, I had a sabbatical and met with him in San Francisco. The plan was for me to stay at his and Tess's house while they went to Europe, but the plans changed. They went to Europe and came back, and were about to go again, when Diane bought this house, so that took care of that plan. We got together again later in the summer after he had just finished "Errand." We went up to Davis, where he read it for the very first time. The next morning we had breakfast with Jack Hicks and some students. He was going to read some of the students' stories and talk with them. We hugged and said good-bye, and that was the last time I saw him. I didn't know that at the time.

How did you hear that he was ill?

He called me up and told me. He told me that he had something dark down there – it was going to be hard business, but it had to be attended to – I'm optimistic, and I'm sure it's going to be fine – it's not my time yet.

I was frightened. But then again, I couldn't imagine anything like that happening to him. What I thought about was that time in New Orleans and how when he was talking about cashing it in early, I kept busting his chops. I had told him he'd better not croak without leaving me something. Well, he did leave me something, more than he ever knew.

Douglas Unger

You said earlier that Ray believed he had become lucky –

Yes, he considered himself fortunate. Even when he was so sick, he reminded himself and everyone else just what he had come back from. When he was going into surgery for lung cancer here at St. Joseph's Hospital, he was joking with us. He said, Well, there was the old life, and then there had been the new life. There he was lying on the gurney, a blue shower cap on his head, prepped for surgery. "Well, I'm on to the next new life," he said as they wheeled him out of the room.

Then in the spring, when they gave him his honorary doctorate in Hartford, he was so happy. He turned to everyone and said, "Well, it's Dr. Carver now. You'll all have to start calling me doctor," he said and laughed. It was just two months before he died. That was really the top for him, even though he was suffering so badly from cancer and had the brain tumor and all the radiation therapy. From Hartford he went on to give a reading at the Endicott bookstore and sign copies of *Where I'm Calling From*. People were spilling out into the street. He was exhausted from the illness and could barely read. It was a short reading. Then he signed books for hours. The next day he was inducted into the American Academy and Institute of Arts and Letters. He was so proud of that, to stand up there and be honored by his peers and admired by the public. It was a miracle to him. Then he went out to the reception and celebrated with so many old friends. The next day there was another book signing at the Scribner's bookstore. I've never seen anything like it. About twenty writers were there signing books, but there were as many people lined up at Ray's table, waiting for a handshake and signature, as you might see in line for a first-run movie. Hundreds of people. He kept turning to me and saying, "Can you believe this? Isn't this just amazing? Who would have thought this?" That was his attitude. He was so proud of all the attention, and he was so good with all those people. Finally, they had to shut the bookstore down. We were out in the street later and there were still people waiting.

How was he able to get through all that?

Well, you see he had managed to convince both the press and his editors that he had beaten his cancer. Up until mid-June, maybe, he had convinced himself, as well as the world, that he had beaten it. When he was asked how he was doing, he'd say, "I'm getting stronger every day."

He touched people at such a personal level –

It really is amazing and wonderful. I've taught Ray Carver in two languages, in the original here and in Spanish in Latin America. So many people all over the world are still just discovering his work. In Buenos Aires there's a bookshop that also serves coffee and sandwiches. They serve a salad called "Carver" and a sandwich called "Cathedral." Ray's on a restaurant menu in Argentina! The "Cathedral" sandwich is cheese and lettuce on white bread – the simplest things. Everybody, it seems, is reading him down there. Even though the book in paperback costs the equivalent of twenty dollars for people earning one or two hundred dollars a month. They're buying it and Xeroxing it and passing it around. And I know this is happening all over the world.

It's so sad to think there will never be another
Carver story.

I'm not so sure of that. There's a play, *Carnations*, that I don't think has been published. There are film treatments he wrote or collaborated on. There must be other writing. Somewhere in this world there's sure to be a box with forgotten manuscripts in it. I'll just bet that one day we'll be seeing stories and poems we've never read before. And there's always the great work he left us. For me, still, every time I read a story or poem by Ray, it's a new experience.

You're not alone there.

Tobias Wolff

Could you tell us about your last visit with Ray?

Yes, he came over to the house for a Christmas celebration. He was then recovering from his operation for lung cancer. A couple of nights earlier he'd been to a party at Stephen Dobyns's house, and he'd been dancing. Everybody thought, Great, Ray's back in the saddle again. So we were in a mood to celebrate. About a week after that I left for Germany for a year and Ray went out west to Washington with Tess. Then the cancer came back. I guess that's the way it works. Ray probably could have informed himself better of how all this was going to go. From what I now understand, the type of lung cancer he had almost always comes back. There are very few cases where it does not. But even while he was about to go into surgery, he took care not to inform himself about this. He practiced what they call denial, and I was and am all in favor of that. It kept his spirits up to think that he was going to be cured. He never let people talk about it when they'd come over to the house. We'd sit around and joke and laugh. He'd laugh and gossip and ignore his sickness. He just wasn't interested in it. I think that was all to the good, because he was able to keep writing. He was able to stay happy and hopeful. When the cancer came back he kept it to himself as much as possible. He wanted to keep working, and he didn't want a flock of mourners descending upon him. Everybody had gathered around him when he got sick in the fall. There was no reason to repeat that. The important thing for him was to get his work done, so he kept it to himself and kept on working. A very brave man.

> *Was this the period when he wrote the poem "What the Doctor Said," which begins with "He said it doesn't look good / he said it looks bad in fact real bad" and ends with "I may even have thanked him habit being so strong."*

Oh yes. He had a very macabre sense of humor and that comes out in that poem too.

Maryann Carver

> *You've said that you and Ray kept communicating even after you and he had separated. Were you able to keep in touch up to the last stages of his illness?*

Yes . . . during the last year he was especially very real, very open, no posing. He made every word, every feeling count. The last time I saw him alive was at the end of April 1988, when he was receiving radiation treatment in Seattle. Chris, our daughter, and her little girls, Windy and Chloe, and

I went down to see him. I had received a letter from him earlier, right after he'd had his surgery, where he had tried to counsel me and advise me how to behave, consolidate property, and so on, now that we were sort of over the hill. When I read that, I thought, Well, speak for yourself. I'm in the middle of all these projects, and I am working very hard. I'm young at heart and have always been an optimist. I was very saddened to read that negative letter, for after all, I thought, that was not the right attitude to fight cancer with.

So I determined when I went down to the Four Seasons in Seattle, where he was taking us all to lunch, that I'd show him. So I got this absolutely stunning outfit from this store in town called A Touch of Class and wore these incredible gold earrings from Turkey that four people in the restaurant complimented me on. A friend said I looked like I'd just stepped out of a Ferrari.

We arrived before he did, so I waited for him up on the balcony, and when he walked in, oh *(sighs)*, it was the most tragic sight I had ever, ever, ever seen. I saw him – his features – only in the middle of his face it was so swollen. He had this big coat on, and a scarf around his neck, and a cap to cover his loss of hair from the radiation treatments. I saw him, and he saw me. He looked at me and tears flooded his eyes, and he said, "If you're not a sight for sore eyes."

But then he managed to put on a real party for the little girls. He was cheerful at lunch and insisted we all have a different dessert. We were a family, thrilled to be together, holding hands as we ate. They all looked at me at the beginning of the meal, so I said grace. I finished by saying, "in Jesus' name." At one time he would have been upset, but he was right in there this time. This was just gorgeous, because Ray was a consummate survivor. If praying would help now, he would pray. When we were together and we'd land in some godforsaken little room temporarily, and I'd ask him jokingly how he could ever survive in this place, he'd pull a little can out of his pocket of roast beef hash or whatever and prepare a lunch for us. He was always going to survive no matter what, and I took heart to see him pray with such gusto. I told him it was important to pray in Jesus' name, because it was the consciousness involved and invoked, as well as the literal instruction of Jesus in the Bible. I said a prayer for his life and health, and we all said amen.

Then we had such a joyous lunch.

Can you remember the date?

April 22, 1988. He was totally, totally honest and real that day, his absolutely sweetest self. He paid us all compliments, compliments meant to last forever. Later that afternoon I gave him a Reiki treatment. He would have scoffed at that too in the past and considered it an idiosyncrasy of mine. Reiki in the first degree is the laying on of hands technique that Jesus used to heal. It was discovered by a Japanese Christian professor after many years of research. Ray laid his head on the palms of my hands. My hands got hot, and I was holding the exact part of his head where he was daily being zapped with radiation treatments. And he absolutely loved lying with his head in my lap, his head in my hands. He kept saying, "This feels so good, oh, this feels so good."

Were you in touch with him at all after that time?

Yes, he called me on our anniversary in June. He wrote me many letters. He sent me books. He sent me this copy of *Where I'm Calling From*. *(She gets a book from the dining room table covered with many pieces of Carver memorabilia)*

Looking back on it all, what would you say about Ray now?

I think Ray did his job in this life. He honored his life goal and became a first-rate writer who is cherished and read all over the world. I am so proud of him and so pleased with his success. Against many odds, but with many boons and lots of love and support, he realized his talent and accomplished his dream.

On a superficial level, he did not want to die, of course. But I think he had written out all his themes and didn't have a whole lot more to say, or he would have stuck around to do it. I think his Higher Self knew when it was time to go – at the very pinnacle of his life as far as his career was concerned. Ray always had a short attention span. He could never stand to be bored.

He liked to move on, even from ostensibly good situations. I think on some higher plane he wanted to move on and do something else.

And always from the day I met him he knew he was going to die young. We always deferred to what he wanted to do, because however tacitly, we both feared he did not have a long time on this earth. For instance, the last ten years of his life. After five treatment centers, he was sober. After a sick and shaky start, he was writing again as well as ever. At that juncture I checked out and let him have his life, to experience all he could, because he was forty then, and who knew how long he had. He always said, "I'm going to die young, but you're going to live to be a mean old lady."

Ray had a great spirit. He was overall a wonderful husband and father, and there were always more smiles than tears. And I have no doubt in my mind or my heart that, bottom line, neither one of us would have missed it for the world.

And, of course, looked at another way, we ended up having that too . . .

Dick Day

Were you able to visit your old friend before he died?

I hadn't seen him in two years when I found out he was dying. I decided to visit him. It's a drive of seven hundred miles from here. I visited him in the big house in Port Angeles about five weeks before he died. He was heavily bloated from the medication, so at first it was difficult to get through to the Ray I knew, but then after two or three minutes it didn't matter and we went on to do the same thing we had always done. We sat out on his deck and told tall tales and bizarre incidents from the past and in the present.

Like old times except for the sorrowful fact that your friend was dying.

We didn't talk about that. In fact, I was so happy to be talking with him, and he seemed so to be talking with me, that the dark side of things almost ceased to exist. Later I wrote an introduction to a play Ray had written as a student here. Part of it deals with that, my last visit with Ray.

May I ask you to read it?

He was astonished at finding himself losing his battle with cancer. Five weeks before he died, I drove to Port Angeles to visit him and Tess. They had just returned from getting married in Reno. A big man in all respects, an imposing figure in his latter years, he'd been whipped by the disease, bloated and made bald by the therapies. As we talked that day, through the evening, and the next day, our main theme was the strangeness of the way things worked out. We told tall tales about the past. We laughed until tears came. Troubles fell away. Within the grotesque figure of the dying man, I clearly saw young Ray just starting out, eleven years behind me, with most of his work dreamed of but still not written. It was a prolonged, enchanted time-out during which, deluded, I said, "To the future." But then, of course, we had to say good-bye.

I am damned glad I went up there, Sam.